Shaping a Personal Myth to Live By

For Mari:
With best wishes
and affection —
Penelope Youngblut

Shaping a Personal Myth to Live By

JOHN R. YUNGBLUT

ELEMENT
Rockport, Massachusetts • Shaftesbury, Dorset

© 1992 John R. Yungblut

Published in the U.S.A. in 1992 by
Element, Inc.
42 Broadway, Rockport, MA 01966

Published in Great Britain in 1992 by
Element Books Limited
Longmead, Shaftesbury, Dorset

Printed in the United States of America by Edwards Brothers

Library of Congress Cataloging-in-Publication Data

Yungblut, John R.
    Shaping a personal myth to live by / John R. Yungblut.
    Includes bibliographical references.
    1. Life. 2. Myth. I. Title.
BD431.Y86 1992
291.1'3—dc20 91-28367

British Library Cataloguing-in-Publication Data

Yungblut, John R.
    Shaping a personal myth to live by.
    I. Title
    253.5

    ISBN 1-85230-278-X

To my beloved wife, Penelope, who carries my projection of her mythological namesake and constitutes in some sense the home to which my inward journey tends.

Contents

Acknowledgements

A Matter of Personal Survival: Life After Death by Michael Marsh. Wheaton, IL: The Theosophical Publishing House, © 1985. Used by permission.

In Defense of Death by M.P. John. Pondicherry, India: Jyotishikha Press, © 1989. Used by permission.

The Heart of Matter by Pierre Teilhard de Chardin. New York: Harcourt Brace Jovanovich, © 1978. Used by permission.

''*Old Age and Death*'' in *Betwixt and Between* by Jane Hollister Wheelwright. LaSalle, IL: Open Cart, © 1987. Used by permission.

The Presence: Poems Nineteen Eighty-Four to Nineteen Eighty-Nine by Kathleen Raine. Hudson, NY: Lindisfarne Press, © 1987. Used by permission.

All biblical references are from the King James version.

Introduction

If we are to communicate with one another about the importance of myth, we shall first have to agree on the sense in which we are using the word. Webster's Dictionary makes helpful distinctions between three ways in which the word is commonly used: myth as "legend"; myth as "poetic fiction"; and myth as "fabulous narrative about about an event in the early period of a people by which they have come to know themselves, their God, and the rest of creation." This latest definition is what theologians, poets, and philosophers use when they speak about religion. Their intent is not to belittle or diminish the tenets of a given religion, but to interpret and to clarify.

The word "faith" is almost synonymous with myth in this context, except that the one who uses the word "faith" is likely to speak in dogmatic terms, while the one who speaks of faith in metaphors, and knows that he or she does so, keeps the myth open-ended, thereby allowing it to evolve and expand. Gordon Alport of the Psychology Department at Harvard, defines faith in this way: "Faith is not the absence of doubt but the will to believe in the presence of doubt." Doubt is the shadow side of faith, its opposite. Belief is the conjunction of these opposites.

Many years ago Robert Frost wrote an article for an educational magazine entitled "Education by Poetry." He said that the only enthusiasm he could tolerate any longer was an enthusiasm which had been tamed by metaphor. He might have entitled his article "Education by Metaphor." It would have amounted to the same thing, for poetry that is bereft of good metaphors and images is not poetry. Metaphor serves both myth and poetry by keeping them open-ended and thereby allowing them to continue to evolve within the consciousness and aesthetic sensibility of men and women.

Metaphor, saying something is "like" something else, prompts active imagination. This invites other additional subtle metaphors of a complementary nature. If one clings to literal understanding of the tenets of any religion, violent conflict may ensue. The most vicious conflicts may arise between the sects of that religion. The different sects claim orthodoxy for their followers and their intransigence can lead to so-called "Holy Wars." Find on a map or geographic globe the place where the most bitter fighting is now taking place. Are these not places where religious fanatics condemn each other and succeed in assuring themselves that they do battle in the name of their God and are thereby made invincible?

On the other hand, when statements of belief are expressed in metaphors, there is nothing to fight about. Appreciation of the metaphorical allows more than one way to express the truth or interpret phenomena. One is encouraged to expand the vision evoked by the metaphor, or to create new ones to illuminate other aspects of the truth. When the person knows that more than one metaphor can allude to the same mysterious truth, he or she is grateful for the richness of the phenomenon to which it points, and may be enlightened by the complementary views of others. C. G. Jung lamented: "Why can't the Church just for once express itself in metaphors instead of the dogmatic statements of a creed which are then made the standards of faith."

There is something wonderful about metaphoric statements which honor the truth that is being described without diminishing its greatness. Only metaphor can do justice to the mystery because the author knows that it is impossible to impart the elusive meaning and numinous power of a reality so profound. Great wisdom is to be found in the judgment of Israel in protecting the indescribable identity of God by insisting that Yahweh shall remain nameless, even "imageless." But it is still legitimate to keep alive the existence and nature of God in metaphorical terms.

Myth and metaphor are the only language that religion can use to point to the ultimate truths. Myth and metaphor bear witness to and protect the truths religion would interpret from appearing dogmatic on the one hand or banal on the other. The great questions persist. For example, scientists talk about an expanding universe, black holes and quasars. But what existed before the big bang that set the galaxies in motion is not known. It is all conjecture.

At a certain point in the infinite regression to the "beginning" active imagination balks. One peers down into the abyss and listens.

There is only an echo of one's own voice. Scientists are reduced to using the same words that reflect the experience of the mystics, reporting on the depths of their experience in contemplative prayer as an encounter with darkness, the void, emptiness, nothingness. How we long to know what happened in the beginning. What constituted the real beginning, if we be not deceived in holding that there was any beginning at all? We imagine what the end will be like if indeed we can conceive any end to the process of evolution. The mind stretches and strains, but we encounter the void and no answer comes.

Will there be personal survival in any recognizable form for individuated psyches? Will anything of our consciousness survive? There are intimations of personal survival but no assurances. If, at death, nothing survives and death spells oblivion for both psyche and soma, how can we bear the futility of all the efforts we put into becoming an individuated self? What kind of God would require this of us? We shall deal with some of these questions later on. For the present, it is enough to acknowledge the existence of questions which haunt our inner journey. We long for answers, but the great mystery remains. It is no wonder we are occasionally depressed. In his autobiography, C.G. Jung says modestly, "Life is full of meaning and meaninglessness. I dare to hope that meaning will preponderate." And Robert Frost says candidly, "I don't know where it's likely to go better." There is in us an inclination to confirm these statements.

There is much to frighten us in outer space and thus far there is no report of sentient life or any other kind of life on other planets. Scientists say that even if in the future we were to discover life on other planets, it would bear little likeness to life as we know it on this planet. Our universe is a lonely place in terms of companionship for human beings. We now know where we are coming from in some detail since life first appeared on this planet. But we do not know the sequence of transformations from the birth of the planet all the way up the scale to the first primitive cells. Teilhard de Chardin, whose vision we shall often refer to in this book, asked if there was a continuity from pre-life to life, and proposed a sequence: subatomic substance to atoms to molecules to heavier, more dense, and more complicated molecules which carried the capacity to become cells. Later on we shall look further into this critical transformation into life from what we would call inanimate matter, a potential for life from the beginning. Astrophysicists are probing space and learning from each adventure into space, manned or unmanned.

With the rapidity with which discoveries are being made, our present myths of creation proposed by scientists may be outdated in a few years. We need to get on with our own personal myths of meaning. C. G. Jung noted that of all the patients that had come to him over thirty-five years of age, every single one of them was suffering from a loss of myth. Without a personal myth of meaning, one is vulnerable to being overwhelmed by a sense of meaninglessness. A myth which one embraces wholeheartedly can be enormously helpful in putting one's life together, thus constellating one's entire life in a pattern of wholeness.

A viable myth, one which continually speaks to the condition of the individual whom it possesses, can afford that individual a steady stream of energy. It can relate to each other the various parts of that person's life, thereby giving them meaning and purpose, drive and effectiveness. It can draw upon resources available in the unconscious, namely the archetypes. It can constitute a bond between that person's unconscious and his or her consciousness. But the myth has to be "reasonable." It has to stand the test of reason, for "reason still is king" as Dean Inge asserts in his book on mysticism. By reasonable I mean that it has to fit the experience of the person and be credible within the context of that person's life. The metaphors must carry weight and appeal, and must be persuasive and convincing.

At the same time, the metaphors have to allow for change and the growth that evolution demands. Good and appropriate metaphors are never to be taken literally. When they are taken literally they demean the reality to which they are pointing. The metaphors which express and give life to the myth can remain useful only by retaining a sort of free-floating tentativeness. They must never attempt to be definitive or final, lest they become idolatrous. A myth to live by must "work" for one; not that it should answer every question put to it by the psyche, but it should help the individual ask the right questions and learn to live with them as the poet Rilke understood. Perhaps the myth is called upon to evolve to meet the needs of the psyche in accommodating some fresh revelation. It may be that the myth must be radically changed to meet the needs of a new perspective that science has revealed as a result of research.

Christianity produced a great myth to meet the needs of the Jewish people at a critical moment, and it has survived twenty centuries. It has dominated all other myths in the West. Nowhere has it been expressed with such prodigious condensation as in the sixteenth verse of the third chapter of the Gospel of St. John: "God so loved the world that he gave his only begotten son to the end that all that believe in him should not perish but have everlasting life."

This "fabulous narrative" inspired the visual artists of the Middle Ages. It moved Dante to write *The Divine Comedy*. For twenty centuries it has dominated the art of western man and woman. Millions of Christians have marched behind the cross in different kinds of processions. This remains one of the great myths of history. There still are millions who cherish this myth and pay homage to its central figures, accepting its tenets on a literal basis. Yet there are indications that the great monolith is cracking in terms of both the solidarity it has enjoyed and its hold over the minds and hearts of its people. Where once there was an unquestioning acceptance in a literal sense of its teachings and credal statements, it has continued to fragment into sects over the last four hundred years.

Karl Jaspers, the German philosopher, has convincingly portrayed what he has called an "axial" period of history: the six hundred years, 800 B.C. to 200 B.C. A phenomenon on the same scale of magnitude as evolution itself took place simultaneously in three separate places on the earth: in Greece, in the Middle East, and in the Far East. The phenomenon had to do with how men and women identify themselves and relate to their culture. Prior to 800 B.C., virtually everyone saw himself or herself as a member of a collective, a race, a nation, a culture, or a religious community. Then something happened with an importance on the scale of evolution in these three places.

In Greece the first systematic philosophers and mathematicians of great stature arose. Aristotle, Socrates, and Plato thought of themselves as more than members of the Greek collective. They were practicing the pursuit of individuation centuries before the birth of C. G. Jung. They thought of themselves as persons with their own identities risking isolation and solitude in order to pursue truths that seemed more sound than the collective ideas put forward by the schools of the time.

In the Middle East the great prophets of Israel, so far from taking as standards the mores of the religious collective to which they belonged, did not hesitate to speak out and castigate the people. They turned to the inner light in the depths of their own hearts to condemn injustice and demand uprightness of their fellow Israelites. Soon Jesus of Nazareth was to join the great procession of which they were the forerunners.

In the Far East the Upanishads, one of the great religious documents of the ages, were written during this period. The Buddha was born in India, and the Buddhist stream of piety spread and evolved, making its own witness to this day. In China the Tao was delineated by Lao-tzu, and Confucius initiated another moral and religious movement.

Ewert Cousins, Professor of Theology at Fordham University in New York and student of the history of spirituality, has proposed that there is now a second axial period. This began with the industrial revolution and continues to gain momentum. It is characteristic of this movement to return to a kind of collective means of identification. This time, however, it is a collective as broad as the species, while at the same time it seeks and promotes the idea of individuation. There is a paradox involved: to think independently as a person and at the same time to think and act globally. Without abandoning the great stride forward in attaining a measure of individuation, we realize that we can no longer live in isolation. We must henceforth recognize that we are "part of the main" in everything we do or say. We must train ourselves to identify globally.

When one of the astronauts stood on the surface of the moon and was able to take a color picture of the earth from 250,000 miles out, we saw in perspective what we looked like, hanging in space, for the first time. It was an awesome experience and a humbling one. It was a visual metaphor that could tame our enthusiasm for our own country. No nations were visible, no boundary lines. Henceforth we were constrained to think globally. If we have any value, it is not as Americans or Europeans, for example, but as human beings, Homo sapiens. We do not know and are not likely to learn for some time whether there is any sentient creature anywhere else in the universe. Our enthusiasm for what it is to be human has been tamed by this visual metaphor. We are precariously hanging in space.

Is this phenomenon unique in the universe? We are all what we are because we were born on the earth. We are of the earth. We are earthlings. There is a direct line of continuity from subatomic particles and stardust to our present sophisticated selves. The earth is our mother and we her children. Matter, the original matter, is still present in our structure. We have endured many transformations. For this reason we are as old as the universe. There is that in us which can claim immortality until now. If this continuity is to survive our death it must be by way of some aspect of consciousness, since the body visibly disintegrates and decays. It may be that the soul is the immortal element that undergoes yet another transformation at death. We shall ponder death and its service to life. For the present, let us see what elements are necessary to include in a viable myth of meaning for our time.

I. *A New Creation Story*

First of all, we need to have a myth of creation. Every story has to have a beginning. Our scientists are coming to accept the big bang theory as the birth of our universe. But there must have been something else before that phenomenon took place. What was the context in which it occurred? Who or what pushed the button that produced the explosion? Who designed how such an explosion took place and created the kind of material that responded to the command? Genesis in the Bible proposes two alternative myths of the six-day creation. But that myth, at least when it is taken in a literal sense, is discredited by the emergence of the revelation of a continuing creation through evolution. Designing an acceptable myth of creation for today would have to come to terms with cosmogenesis, a universe still being born.

The author of the Book of Ecclesiastes firmly announces that "there is no new thing under the sun." But from time to time, whole new species of creatures appear under the sun, not to speak of events that are wholly new under the sun. Ecclesiastes does allow that "time and chance happeneth to all men," alluding to the fact that new things are happening in the lives of men and women every day. Given the discovery of the fact of evolution and the new theories that have to do with space and time, what kind of creation myth can be consistent with all that we are learning about our universe today?

II. *The New Image of the Anthropos*

The second element that a viable myth of meaning must contain is some assessment of the value of man and woman; an image of the Anthropos. What is it to be man or woman, and what is our place in creation? As a reference point against which any contemporary myth of man and woman must be measured, one recalls the Biblical query and response, "What is man that thou art mindful of him and the son of man that thou visitest him? Thou has made him a little lower than the angels and hast crowned him with glory and honor.'' (Psalms 8:4–5) Possibly our contemporary counterpart to the theory would be expressed something like this: "Thou hast endowed him with intellect, moral perception and creative potential.'' But, to be honest, we should have to acknowledge the presence in him of the shadow, his capacity for evil individually and corporately. Our myth of meaning would have to recognize the negative as well as the positive potential in us.

In weighing the condition of man and woman, we shall have to consider the need of modern man and woman to be saved from themselves and their evil impulses. We would have to reassess the traditional myth that we are saved by Jesus' death upon the cross, if we are followers of the way. Our Christology will have to be rewritten, and we shall have to see Jesus in the light of evolution. The lines of our Christology will have to begin "to follow that curve," as the great Jesuit paleontologist and philosopher Teilhard de Chardin expressed it.

III. *The Development of the Mystical Faculty*

The third article in a new statement of faith might well be related to the mystical element. The Religious Society of Friends puts it this way: "There is that of God in every man and woman." In my own myth I want to extend the claim to be more inclusive. There is that of God in everything, what Teilhard calls "the diaphany of the divine at the heart of matter" itself. God is immanent as well as transcendent. In India it is said that Atman (God within) is Brahman. In Buddhism, the Buddha is held to be in everyone. Christianity has had its mystical strain, "an apostolic succession of mystics," many of whom were excommunicated. The Muslim faith gave rise to another apostolic succession through the Sufi sect. The myth we are shaping in this book, the diaphany of God at the heart of matter, Teilhard's numinous phrase, is a perception that can only be made with the mystical consciousness by one who has contemplated this evolving faculty in man and woman. Judaism in the Cabala, and in modern times in the Hassidic movement, deliberately cultivated the mystical consciousness, primarily in Eastern Europe. Mysticism is a form of religious experience that lies at the heart of all the great living religions.

The mystical strain which is present in the evolutionary secular humanism is always suspect by the authorities and abhored by the institutionalists because it threatens the establishment and recognizes only one authority: the voice that speaks through inner mystical experiences. Our new concern for the well-being of the earth needs to find itself expressed in a new evolutionary mysticism. Mystical union with the earth and its creatures, such as the first Americans knew and practiced, is a spirituality of the earth itself, growing out of the earth, the earth's own spirituality. We have much to learn from others in this regard.

Another aspect in a viable myth of meaning is a new relationship to other living religions. Douglas Steere has a lovely phrase to signify the new opportunity for the creative impact upon each other: "mutual irradiation." The way forward to a new world religion, Arnold Toynbee said, is not to try to put together an eclectic religion by borrowing a little here and a little there. What he prophesied is that the religion of tomorrow will be that religion among the living religions which proves itself so capable of expanding its myth and creating new and viable metaphors that those coming to it from other religions will find that they have lost nothing of value. He dared to hope that Christianity might be the one chosen for this unification. But I am told that in the end he indicated that Sufism might be attempting this task more effectively than Christianity is able to do at this time.

There are more and more colloquia that bring together contemplatives representative of the different living religions. At the moment it would seem that Buddhist and Christian contemplatives have the most to say to each other.

Several summers ago I was invited to attend a conference sponsored by the Naropa Institute in Boulder, Colorado. Trungpa, leader of the Institute, and the Dalai Lama were among those present. The purpose of this particular gathering was to contemplate or meditate, as the Buddhists would say, twice a day and to share what we could of the nature of the experience itself. We were not to talk about theological differences but to focus on the experience of contemplative prayer. The contemplative experience was the bridge between us, the bond that brought us together and the commitment that would keep us together. A book was developed from that conference, *Speaking of Silence*, edited by Susan Walker. There have been follow-up conferences each summer since.

There have been more and more interfaith conferences summoned to bring together contemplatives concerned about social issues as well. The Temple of Understanding has been instrumental in this movement. These two areas of shared interests, prayer and social action, have had the most successful dialogue, but mutual concerns and mutual irradiation have also been apparent at the different meetings. The affinities are becoming more and more viable and audible. It is clear that what these religious bodies evoke when they come together is also what they have in common. A growing trust is developing among the contemplatives of all the living religions.

IV. *The Eternal Feminine*

None of the current revolutionary movements is more far reaching than the sexual revolution. We shall designate the fourth factor to be considered the eternal feminine. The Feminist Movement is responsible for the many vigorous forms the sexual revolution has taken; the demand for equality in ministry, theology, job opportunities, the political arena, and in what is called "inclusive language." The "God is dead" movement would seem to have languished, the demand to have feminine pronouns for deity on an equality basis has not. Books containing masculine pronouns referring to God are doomed to criticism for this reason alone. This has cut a wide swath in what is considered appropriate. God must be androgynous or feminine as a kind of compensatory reaction, or an "affirmative action," in theological terms.

There is no doubt that there has been gross injustice in this area of theology, and amends must be made. The relevant question is how to accomplish this without creating a discontinuity that threatens the sense of the historical continuity. The Liberation Movement has been stimulated by the Feminist Movement. Various leaders of the movement claim that the Bible must be rewritten along with the Hymnal and the Book of Common Prayer in order to meet this requirement. The movement that calls itself "The Third World Liberation Movement" wants virtually the whole of theology re-written.

There is a certain demand for equality that is wholly justified. How to preserve the good elements in the Church's history and at the same time make amends where this is indicated is still an unresolved problem. There is a danger that if all the demanded changes are met in the Bible, Hymnal, and Prayer Book, and the demands of full equality of the various institutional power struggles for equal representation are also met, new problems will still arise. For example, the "vigilante" groups might realize that equality in principle has been achieved and conceded, yet new quarrels in competition might arise. One young female priest put it this way, "We have the priesthood now, but all the best parishes and the highest salaries go to the male priests." I am sure that she was speaking from experience. It remains true, however, that anyone who would shape a sound myth to live by will want to have this principle adhered to: equality of the sexes. The Church has suffered from male chauvinism too long.

Closely related to the Feminist Movement is the whole question of the relationship between sexuality and spirituality. It was Teilhard's conviction that sexuality is the primary agent that fuels the spiritual. Far from being a distraction from the spiritual focus, the sexual can channel its energy. It is the primary energy available to spirituality. "Spirituality descends upon the dyad, not the monad." Teilhard confesses that he had never achieved a synthesis of his insights apart from relationship to a woman. There is no question that he was faithful to his vow of celibacy. He deliberately and consciously sublimated his sexual energy in the service of his spirituality. The energy derived from his restrained sexuality was put to work in the development of his quest for wholeness.

He wrote an essay on the evolution of chastity. He knew that the sexual urges to expression were, next to the spiritual, the most powerful drive in the psychosomatic unity that is in man and woman. Unless it can be guarded over, it may become a pretender to the throne, drawing other sources of energy into its orbit. The only other energy that is more potentially powerful is the instinctual energy under the direction of the religious urge in the psyche to "get it all together."

In an essay entitled "The Feminine, or the Unitive" Teilhard describes how, in dialogue with a woman, a man is enabled to see the way ideas can come together. Just as woman can preside over the social gathering that relates people to one another, so can she help man relate ideas to one another. When the anima calls for recognition and scope for herself in the heart of a man's psyche, then the same ministry of the feminine may take place within.

V. *On Living Into the Forgiven Life*

There is one article of doctrine which deserves a special place in the myth. We shall place it fifth on our list. It has to do with the role of forgiveness in any viable myth of meaning. Several years ago, while reading the poetry of William Blake, I came to a poem called "The Everlasting Gospel." There was a prose preface in which Blake asked the question, "Was there anything new in the teaching of Jesus, anything that had not been anticipated by any of the ancients like Plato or Cicero for example?" His own answer to this important question was immediate and confident, "Only one thing—the importance Jesus attached to the forgiveness of sins." I had never thought of this emphasis before, and went straight to the gospels to verify this claim. To my surprise I had to admit that Blake's statement was true. Do you know how we take a simple word sometimes and quite arbitrarily attach to it a new weight of meaning? The innocent little preposition "into" is a case in point. We say someone is "into knitting," or "into gardening," or "into fishing," meaning that he or she is consumed with a passionate interest in the practice. What I concluded from my studies and what I had to confess when I listened to the teachings of Jesus was that he, regardless of whatever else fascinated him or he thought important, was *into* forgiveness in a big way! It has led me since to further reflection which I shall share later in the book. For the present, suffice it to say that the great importance of the phenomenon of forgiveness entitled it to a special place in my own myth of meaning to live by.

VI. *Intimations of Immortality*

The last element in the quest for a myth of meaning that demands assessment and formulation is what we believe about the possibility of life after death. After the age of seventy, most individuals are somewhat preoccupied with thoughts of death. Close friends are passing. One's own death is inevitably creeping up a pace. All sorts of unfamiliar emotions are expressing themselves. There are few who are concerned about the old question of whether one will be assigned to heaven or hell. In a universe which we have come to know a little more about, our anxiety has often more to do with whether we can anticipate survival in any form at all.

Obviously no part of the body survives. We know so much about the psychosomatic unity that it is hard to see how there can be survival of any part of the soul or consciousness. And without consciousness what continuity of personhood could there be? Many are pinning their hopes on reports of persons who claim to have passed over to the other side. There are mediums who purport to be able to put one in touch with a loved one now deceased. There are claims of communicating by channeling with loved ones who have been long dead. There is the purported belief in reincarnation. I would like to believe in some of these after death experiences, but I must confess that it seems to me that these psychic experiences could well be accounted for in terms of the collective unconscious.

My own inclination is to place more confidence in mystical experiences permitted by the collective unconscious. My own ''intimations of immortality'' have been incidents of an experience of eternity, timelessness, hints of a divine presence within my own psyche. Nonetheless, I feel I must commit my soul and body to the Holy in utter trust in that person or process to whom or to which I owe my life in the great mystery. I am trying to learn to trust the universe and its God to make whatever disposition they wish of the entity I now am. Yea, though God assign me to oblivion, yet will I love God.

Let us now begin to ponder more deeply all the elements we have proposed for inclusion in a viable myth to live by.

CHAPTER ONE

A New Creation Story

There is no part of our traditional Christ myth that needs more radical revision than the creation story. The six day creation story, two versions of which are given in Genesis, is no longer tenable. We can no longer speak of a cosmology. To be true to the facts that we know, we must now speak of a cosmogenesis; a cosmos still being born, a process of continuing creation through evolution. Despite the fact that there are thousands of fundamentalists who believe in the Genesis stories and call their faith ''creationism'' there is no scientific support of a reputable kind for these ancient stories.

There may be support in many quarters for the ''big bang'' theory of the origin of the universe as we now have it, galactic systems and all. There seems to exist a general support of the so-called black hole theory as it is now interpreted. But there is always the question of what was there before the big bang came. Granted, everything seemed to dance into the present configuration physically at that time. But this pushes anything that has to do with the ultimate beginning further and further into the past, the ultimate beginning of which we cannot even imagine.

Teilhard says that henceforward we must see everything in terms of biological space-time or duration. Up until now space has been the more important factor, but from now on time will be even more important. When contemplating aspects of evolution it is time, time that matters most. Time is more important than space in determining the relationship and the impact of one creature upon another because space in relation to habitat is always changing. The emergence of life and the trace of life in creation relates far more to time. The reactions and impacts of one species upon another have more to do with synchronistic convergences than spatial considerations. Biological space-time or duration has more to do with whether one species flourishes and another declines in a given habitat.

Teilhard's Contribution

That creation continues, (incidentally also the title of a book by Fritz Kunkel a generation ago), and that we can watch it taking place and cooperate as co-creators, have been a tremendous revelation. It is comparable in importance to the discoveries of Galileo and Copernicus in the impact that such a discovery may have on man and woman. In attempting to gauge the importance of Darwin's discoveries, we must realize that they were on the scale of this magnitude. When Teilhard was questioned about the importance of the discovery of the fact of evolution, he chose to respond in two striking metaphors: "Evolution is a fact illuminating all other facts. It is a curve which all lines must henceforth follow." The lines of all of the sciences must follow this curve if their work indeed is to be thinkable and true. I do not believe that this judgment is excessive.

Many may well be familiar with the facts of Teilhard's life, but it may be important to introduce him once more for the sake of those who are not. He was born in the Auvergne section of France in 1881. The fourth of eleven children, he showed early signs of unusual curiosity and sensitivity in responding to the wonder and beauty of nature. At the age of five he chose iron as his God. The criteria he applied were durability and consistency. When, at the age of six or seven he learned that iron rusted, he flung himself on the grass and wept the most bitter tears of his life. Undaunted, he pursued his quest. His book, *The Heart of Matter*, is an autobiographical sketch in which he tells us that he wants to show how:

> starting from the point at which the spark was first struck, a point that was built into me congenitally, the World caught fire for me, burst into flames; how this happened all during my life, and as a result of my whole life, until it formed a great luminous mass, lit from within, that surrounded me.
>
> Crimson gleams of Matter gliding imperceptibly into the gold of Spirit, ultimately to become transformed into the incandescence of a Universe that is Person—and through all this there blows, animating it and spreading over it as a fragrant balm, a zephyr of Union and of the Feminine.

The Diaphany of the Divine at the heart of a glowing Universe as I have experienced it through contact with the Earth—the Divine radiating from the depth of a blazing Matter: this it is that I shall try to disclose and communicate in what follows.

As a child Teilhard had a "sense of plenitude," the "sense of consummation and of completion: the Pleromic Sense." When he was disillusioned he looked for something that could take the place of iron as his personal symbol for God. He tried the blue flame hovering over the logs of the hearth, quartz or amethyst crystals, and fragments of chalcedon. Note that the qualifications included resistance. "The substance chosen should be resistant, impervious to attack and hard," like quartz. He sought "a sort of universal root or matrix of being."

So it was that the Sense of Consistence led to the awakening and expansion of a dominant and triumphant Sense of the Whole.

He was sent to a boarding school, run by the Society of Jesus. He developed a passionate interest in geology, the "science of stones." Then came physics, which he later taught in Cairo. About this time he substituted "the new and the rare" for "the solid and the incorruptible." Finally he came to the position he describes for us:

I no longer doubted but that the supreme happiness I had formerly looked for in Iron was to be found only in spirit.

He shares with us the sequence of discoveries in his quest for an adequate image of God. He tells us:

The 'piece of iron' of my first days has long been forgotten. In its place it is the Consistence of the Universe, in the form of Omega Point, that I now hold, concentrated (whether above me, or, rather, in the depths of my being, I cannot say) into one single indestructible centre WHICH I CAN LOVE.

Teilhard's concept of Point Omega and his identification of Point Omega with the Christ figure was finally to take its shape in the exalted Christology which he offered in the essay entitled "The Christic" in *The Heart of Matter*. Those ideas, together with others, brought on the disfavor of his superiors and as a result, he was in deep trouble. His presence was desired in Rome for interrogation, the first in a series of visits which consistently found him approaching heresy. He was considered dangerous and was prohibited from lecturing on, or publishing, anything philosophical or theological the rest of his life. It was a severe blow, but he felt it necessary to be obedient. Some friends tried to persuade him to leave the Jesuit order and seek a liberal bishop, perhaps in Holland, who would accept him and grant him freedom from the kind of inquisition he was undergoing. But he declined to follow this advice, saying that he had taken the vows of the Society of Jesus and that he intended to remain a loyal Jesuit, no matter what the cost.

I have sometimes wondered what he would have done if the demand had been that he stop writing as well. The most satisfying explanation that I have heard is that Teilhard was a French aristocrat by background and a "gentleman keeps his word." He was also fond of saying that the Society of Jesus was his divine milieu and he would not leave it.

Meanwhile the woman into whose hands he committed his theological and philosophical writings, Jeanne Mortier, not a member of any order, and not under the constraint of obedience, either translated his works or saw that they were translated. According to their prior agreement she brought them out in sequence after his death. Pope John XXIII, in keeping with his generous nature, ordered the writings put on the table for study at the time of Vatican II. "If they contain falsehood we will know it sooner or later, and if they contain truth we need to be informed."

Recall that Teilhard had been forbidden to lecture or publish on anything theological or philosophical from his early thirties until he died. But his scientific work was much appreciated by paleontological and geological colleagues. Teilhard had done the basic work that led to the discovery of Peking man. As a geologist he won the respect that brought him world recognition as a scientist.

Teilhard, according to Julian Huxley, achieved a three-fold synthesis of the material and physical world with the world of mind and spirit. It was a synthesis inclusive of the past with the future, of variety with unity, of the many and the one. While Huxley confessed that he did not follow Teilhard's reasoning in relation to future prophesy, he conceded the brilliance of Teilhard as a scientist. This was high praise from one of the giants in the scientific community.

Teilhard died in New York City in 1955. He had told his friends he wanted to die on Easter Day, and so he did. It was his way of "living your dying," a potent metaphor.

No one has contributed more to a new myth of meaning, especially in the part of the myth that would have to do with creation. He gave a name to the new story, the new creation myth: cosmogenesis. His

Jesuit education spoke of cosmology. Thomas Aquinas was the great theologian who had been educated in the scholastic school of eternal verities patterned after Aristotle's philosophy. But in his science classes he was learning about the new world of constant change at the patient pace of evolution. Thomas Aquinas drew distinctions between matter and spirit. In Teilhard's new evolving universe they revealed themselves as two sides of one coin. When Teilhard turned to one of the priests in seminary who taught science and confessed that he was puzzled, he told us he was given the best counsel he had ever received. Teilhard was to follow the revelation of science and hold onto theological dogmas only if they were compatible with science. Teilhard put it this way:

> If, as a result of some interior revolution, I were successfully to lose my faith in Christ, my faith in a personal God, my faith in the Spirit, I think that I would still continue to believe in the World. The World (the value, the infallibility, the goodness of the World): That in the final analysis, is the first and last thing in which I believe.

This was a bold statement at the time. It was a commitment to which he was to hold fast until the end. For Teilhard research became, as he said, a prayer of adoration. If he discerned a conflict between his science and his inherited theology, the theology must give way. No one has contributed more to reconciling science and religion than Teilhard. This is an additional reason why Teilhard's thoughts about a new myth of meaning should be taken seriously. He was shaping his own myth of meaning.

What exactly was Teilhard's personal myth of meaning? The novice master had encouraged him to be consistent. Truth is one. Teilhard was wary of materialists who were not sufficiently disciplined in the scientific research. Moreover, he was beset early on by two anxieties. He said that many modern men and women were suffering from the "malady of space-time." At the same time his query concerned whether there would be a "suitable outcome to evolution." Was it going anywhere? Did it have any goal or purpose? Faithful to the end to the scientific approach, he resolved to "follow the lines passed by evolution until they achieve their maximum coherence." He did so and nature once again revealed her secrets.

What *was* revealed to him was the direction in which evolution was moving. "The axis of forward movement could be called complexity consciousness." As evolution continued, its creatures became more and more complex and at the same time moved toward greater consciousness. This observation satisfied him as to purpose and also led him to see that there was an underlying goal. Evolution was going somewhere, to a distant goal of higher consciousness. In Teilhard's mind there is then both direction and destination in the process of evolution. Indeed, the Feminist Movement had the right words for it, "consciousness raising." The phrase can be applied to the whole process. Below the level of sentience on the tree of life we can speak of complexification. Above the level of sentience we must add the word consciousness so the process becomes complexity consciousness. Consciousness enormously enhances and intensifies the complexity. At the center of consciousness there is the mysterious code that has the promise of rising consciousness.

There is another point in Teilhard's vision that constitutes one of his basic insights in his own myth of meaning. It has to do with what he called "the within of things" in contrast with the "without of things." Science up to now has been engaged in describing and measuring the "without" of things. But there is also the "within" of things. It is precisely in this mystery that the code of potential for evolutionary change and development exists. For this study there needs to be a highly developed and well-organized team of scientific men and women.

There is an interesting and amusing story that illustrates Teilhard's vision at this point. A woman was visiting her analyst for the first time. Note that there is no disparagement of woman here. On the contrary, only a woman would have been capable of this insight. She said to the analyst, "Doctor, I know what is upholding the universe." He responded with that studied composure and enigmatic tone therapists cultivate, "And what is that, madam?" The woman answered with assurance, "A turtle." Without betraying any surprise, the analyst then asked, "What, pray, is upholding the turtle?" The woman replied with a knowing expression on her countenance, "Why, another turtle." Then, as if trying to put pressure gently on the unconscious of the patient, the analyst queried his patient once again. "And what, if you please, is upholding that second turtle?" The woman paused at this point, then feeling supreme confidence in her vision and deep compassion for the ignorance of the analyst, said, "Doctor, it's turtles all the way down."

What Teilhard has been trying to say as a result of his insight, into the nature of matter and spirit was, "It's spirit all the way down into the heart of matter." This constituted a radical change when compared with the earlier doctrine that there was conflict between matter and spirit. Teilhard had become certain that the contrary was true as a result of his research and reflection. The fact of evolution attests from every point of view that creation was not completed in six days. Rather, it is continuing, even now. The continuity since life emerged on this planet is true also between pre-life and life. Indeed the beginning of creation must go back to the beginning of the universe, if we can speak of any beginning at all. From the beginning, at the heart of matter, there has dwelt spirit, awaiting from moment to moment, in the fullness of time, the successive stages by which it was possible to be transformed. Spirit eventually emerged from the womb of matter. Spirit, it may be, is a subtle form of matter.

I believe that this new myth of creation, beginning with the evolutionary process, is the most persuasive hypothesis that has come into the mind of man and woman. It does not explain the very beginning for which not one scientist or poet has discovered the answer or the words. The Bible has the most plausible account, ''In the beginning, God.''

An Indian and Vietnamese View

I have corresponded with an Indian Anglican priest who has continued to publish a little paper called *New Times Observer* for twenty-five years. His name is M. P. John. He came to Pondicherry many years ago, drawn by the thought of Sri Aurobindo, who did for philosophical thought in India what Teilhard has done for Western philosophers and religious thought: assimilate the truth of evolution. He did this with the same passion and conviction that characterized Teilhard. M. P. John came to sit at Aurobindo's feet and ever since Aurobindo's death has continued to interpret his thought, adding his own peculiar perspective and genius. Recently he sent me some copies of his latest book, *In Defense of Death*. Toward the end of his book he shares a poem or poetic creed he wrote on evolution:

> I believe
> in the Principle of Evolution,
> the Maker of heaven and earth
> and the evolving man.

> I believe
> the World Teachers
> built us roads to tread,
> and withdrew to help
> from other planes.
>
> I believe
> they beckon us
> ˙to scale the heights,
> mental and supramental,
> and meet them
> on the Mount of Transfiguration.
>
> I believe
> we shall all evolve
> and be New Beings
> who need no Death
> to take off on wings of Joy
> to worlds without end.

In another place he writes:

Evolution of consciousness is what should engage our attention.

In the beginning was the Principle of Evolution and the Principle of Evolution was God. All things were made by Evolution and without Evolution was not anything made that was made. In Evolution was Life, and the Life was the light of men.

Today it becomes necessary to think of God in terms of Evolution. The life that is in each of us is the manifestation of Evolution, the God within us.

M. P. John is not a well-known figure on the world scale, but his personal myth of meaning is very strong and relevant. We can see what the impact of Sri Aurobindo has done to his thinking. It has transformed his Indian ''ascent.'' The book written by Sri Aurobindo is called *The Life Divine*. It is an epic poem written with a world perspective. He studied at Cambridge, England, and had what one might call a global perspective. He was a gentle man with a world vision. He was a world citizen with a global approach to everything he touched. He wanted to build a world community. It was to be called Auroville. Though it did not realize the dimensions, national or spiritual, that he envisioned, it was indeed a prophesy still to be fulfilled.

Another world citizen who has a global view is Thich Nhat Hanh: poet, philosopher, theologian. He is Vietnamese, another person who transcends the Zen Buddhist faith in which he was brought up. For the Zen Buddhist God is also nameless and imageless. The initiate is to arrive at Satori or enlightenment through meditation. God is not a person but reality itself. Nhat has written a book entitled *The Miracle of Mindfulness* which deals with maintaining simultaneous levels of consciousness. One is an ego-consciousness, concerned with what is going on, and the other is a kind of raised consciousness concurrent with this particular task "under the aspect of the eternal." Perhaps this latter kind of consciousness is characteristic of the individual who has earned the right to be a co-creator with the God of the universe. For this Buddhist, the God of creation is continuously in the act of creating, although this creator would not be called God.

C. G. Jung and Creation

C. G. Jung accepted the Judaeo-Christian concept of the God of creation. That is to say he did not hesitate to use the word God, but his images of God make some radical additions. God is associated not only with grace and glory, but with the creation of evil. God has a dark side. There are passages in Jung where God needs man to raise his or her consciousness. Evil, since it is incorporated into a mandala or a quaternity, along with the historic Trinity, could be said to have a kind of divine sanction. In *Answer to Job*, the devil and God cooperate in the testing of Job.

Job, as Jung sees the story, is a psychological necessity. He had been living in a myth that held, as part of its doctrine, that the good prosper and the evil suffer. Job had the courage to counter this prevailing myth with the conviction that there are exceptions to the rule, notably his own case. Job searches his experience for justification for his own predicament, the suffering that plagued his life. It was clear to him that his punishment did not fit the crime. Clearly, goodness did not automatically produce happiness and good fortune.

Job's friends taunted him with accusations. He must have deserved the suffering which was imposed upon him. This was the orthodox view. Perhaps, they protested, Job is suffering because of his secret sins. We would say, sins repressed into the unconscious of which Job has no memory. They are called secret sins precisely because Job has no conscious memory of them.

Jung in *Answer to Job* gives the impression that he thinks it is God whose consciousness needs to grow. There is one scriptural passage (Isaiah 45:7) which seems to support Jung's conviction that God must be held responsible for the presence of evil in the divine economy: "Behold I create good. I also create evil." The author of this passage perhaps was speaking out of his own experience, or at least out of his own insight. In any case the author of the Book of Job is testifying that Job's experience cries out for revision of this part of the current myth. "Look," he is saying, "this part of our current myth of meaning doesn't hold water." He boldly rebukes those who adhere to the collective view and implies that Job is to be commended, despite his suffering, because of the courage he displayed in his faithfulness and obedience. Job is presented as an archetype of realized individuation.

I do not follow Jung when he seems to imply that Job is instructing God. Jung seems to credit Job with raising God's consciousness. I am not quite sure what Jung is saying here, but his assertion that God's growth seems dependent on Job's raised consciousness I cannot accept. Rather, I see the situation as a transformation of Job's experience of the Holy or God. Job is growing in his personal myth of meaning, not God. God, to be God, must be immutable, unchanging, omniscient, unnamable.

It has been said that after Job, the advent of Jesus was a psychological necessity. I understand this to mean that the Hebrew people had to see for themselves, not by prophetic understanding of the event, but experientially. There is no doubt that some of the people still could not understand when Jesus was actually with them. With the advent of one whom many interpreted as being the Son of God, they would have needed to accept the reverse of the historic doctrine. The Son of God, in whom no one found any wrong, is singled out as one who must undergo the most painful suffering. No one, after witnessing the passion of Jesus on the cross, could hold that there was a direct relationship between sin and suffering. A good man could suffer the crucifixion. The long held proposition, so fully accepted for so long, had to go. Job had led the way. There is no correlation between goodness and any reward in this life and the life to come. The Hebrew consciousness was growing. The Jewish people had to be shown this truth by the experience of a living man, the Jesus of history.

So the children of Israel had to grow in consciousness by the grace of the God they knew and loved. The lesson for Israel was that the "fabulous narrative" had once more to evolve to allow the most righteous one of all to suffer death on the cross at God's command and intention. In this way they could come to a new consciousness of the nature and will of God. The collective judgment is held "wrong again." And the solitary soul who wants only to grow in understanding is granted his or her wish.

There is a lesson here for the sons and daughters of God. The righteous do not always prosper, nor do the evil infallibly suffer for their wrongdoing in this life. In an interview days before his death, Jung was asked who his God was. He made reply in these striking words:

> To this day God is the name by which I designate all things which cross my willful path violently and recklessly, all things which upset my subjective views, plans, and intentions and change the course of my life for better or for worse.

Jung introduces the idea of synchronicity or "meaningful coincidences" into a new creation story. This would extend retrogressively back in time to the very beginnings of the universe. The earth was created "in the fullness of time." The galaxy came together, not fortuitously but synchronistically, when the stars were in a certain position.

It is curious that currently the scientists are being turned to for the writing of a new creation myth more than are the theologians. This is one of the ways in which former antagonistic groups, scientists and theologians, are now listening to each other. Their motivations are different. Scientists now find it relevant to conjecture about the beginning in order to be guided in the quest of present meaning. Theologians are open and listening because they are jealous of any who would invade that territory. Witness such books as *The Tao of Physics* by Fritjof Capra and *The Dancing Wu Li Masters* by Gary Zukav.

The Witness of Matthew Fox

One would want to add to the list *The Universe is A Green Dragon* by Brian Swimme and *Original Blessing* by Matthew Fox. Witness the warm way in which so many church people have received *Original Blessing* whose purpose, among other things, is to downplay the age old emphasis on salvation theology to the benefit of creation theology. In order that the Christian heritage may retain some measure of balance in its presentation to the world, they declare that there should be much positive emphasis on the celebrative rather than on the lugubrious focus on salvation. We must look to the positive elements in the historical Christian heritage in order to compete with the positive and joyous notes now emanating from evolutionary humanism. This, incidentally, was one of the concerns of Teilhard, who believed that there was an unfortunate appeal in contemporary humanism that he coveted for the Christian Church.

The first article in the new myth of meaning for our day must be a remythologizing of our ancient creation myth. The current interest in Matthew Fox and his ideas bespeaks a felt need in this direction by lay people. Matthew Fox is considered heretical and exhibitionist by others. He is dramatic in his presentation, but that is a matter of style, nothing else. He is thereby getting the message across. The fact is that he is striking a responsive note in many who have had to abandon the ancient myth in the name of integrity. The truth is that for a great many people the inherited myth of creation, that the Church has maintained for nearly two thousand years, is not living and surviving as a viable myth. It is still capable of maintaining the loyalty of some who are able to live in two worlds at the same time. But for those for whom it must be one world or none at all, it has been necessary to abandon it and engage in the quest for a new myth. I believe that Teilhard has given us the best statement of a new and viable creation myth of meaning until others arise that are more appealing or more plausible. I am content to work with Teilhard's vision until I am presented with another, still more comprehensive one.

CHAPTER TWO

The New Image of the Anthropos

When the question was put forth in the Old Testament, "What is man that thou art mindful of him and the son of man that thou visitest him," the answer was given, "Thou hast made him a little lower than the angels, and hast crowned him with glory and honor." (Psalms 8:4-5) This was the image of the Anthropos (the whole man) entertained by the Children of Israel as they reflected on the ultimate value of man and woman. Their prophets were not afraid to portray how the children of God betrayed their opportunity in the Garden of Eden and were punished for their wrongdoing. The Christian Church later seized upon this incident in shaping its corporate myth of meaning, its "fabulous narrative." Endowed with the gift of paradise, Adam and Eve belie their trust. At a test of the devil, represented by the snake, they deny their heritage by disobedience. They eat of the fruit from the tree of the knowledge of good and evil and are banished from the garden. The veil of innocence falls from their eyes and, behold, something they had not known before, they are naked. This seems to link sexuality with associations of evil and the implicit judgment has darkened the Church's attitude toward sex ever since.

The Fall in the Garden

In the light of the revelation of the earth as an evolving planet, the "fabulous narrative" must be radically remythologized. In the perspective of evolution, eating of the fruit of the tree which bears the knowledge of good and evil, far from being the source of evil in the world, is a quantum leap forward in human evolution. It represents an enormous gain in raised consciousness. It is the bestowal of moral responsibility and discernment. The ancient response must be radically remythologized and reworked before it can serve as a viable element in a new myth of meaning. Perhaps the statement would come out something like this:

> Thou hast made them a little lower than the angels, and hast crowned them with glory and moral responsibility and the interior perception to deal with opposites in the quest of the self and the raised consciousness that permits the building of individuation.

The work of Freud and Jung on the unconscious has forever altered our appraisal of the value of the Anthropos, man and woman. Though the problem of the presence of evil in a universe as complex as ours is still unresolved, its essence is, succinctly stated, how can a God who is both all powerful and all good have created a universe in which evil is so rampant. It all but begs the question to point out that without evil there could be no good, and that without good evil has no meaning.

Religion is the impulse or instinct to "get it all together." "Religio religare" are the Latin words for "binding into one bundle or sheaf," thereby defining the process of integration, which is moving toward individuation. Binding into one sheaf is the objective of both analysis and religion. When Jung was asked, in an interview with the BBC, about evil in the future and what brought on evil, Jung spoke with a tone of finality. "Man will be responsible for all future evil in the world." "He spoke with authority and not as one of the scribes." What is the devil but that in ourselves which projects on the figure of the historic archetype the dark evil within ourselves. We pin the blame on this pitiable figure because we are unwilling to bear the weight of it. Jung is unwilling for us to dodge our responsibility for evil on the pretense that evil is from the devil.

New Evaluation of Anthropos

The new concept assumes a noble image for man and woman. They are now required to carry the burden themselves, and the appropriate guilt. We do not know why we are so beset within by the Tempter and a miserable proclivity to sin. But we know that it is so. Moreover, we know through Jungian psychology that, just as there deepens a desire or inspiration in us to lead a holy life, a compensatory temptation arises in the psyche of a negative kind. Jung called this the "shadow." The greater the aspiration toward holiness, the more potent and inflammable the devil-like counterpart. Paul had an amazing grasp of the phenomenon: "The good that I would I do not, but the evil which I would not, that I do." (Romans 7:19) Therein lies the deepest mystery. Just when we think we have gotten the better of a bad habit it takes us by surprise and we are undone.

Jung has helped us see that the only viable holiness of life is wholeness of life. Any other notion of taking heaven by storm is illusory. The Anthropos is seen in a different light when one takes into account the unconscious where reside both heaven and hell, God, and the devil. Not the devil of whom we have heard, but a complex in the psyche that would undo our best resolves. Religion, as we were observing a short while ago, is the compulsion, the energy to move in the direction of wholeness. It will not rest until integrity is attained. Jung assigned to religion the task of integrating the contents of the unconscious with those of consciousness if one would attain the Self. To do so, one must cultivate the contemplative in one's self.

If Teilhard is right, that raised consciousness is the goal of evolution, (and one can certainly make a strong case for this), then the Anthropos carries within the secret of the universe. From the very beginning, the possibility of the ultimate arrival of the Anthropos was coded into the heart of matter. We speak of the inner journey by which the Anthropos can be manifested in the individuated man and woman. But there is also the importance of seeing in Anthropos the potential of even further growth in the evolutionary sense. Why should the evolution of sentience cease with the image of the Anthropos? Loren Eiseley in *The Immense Journey* writes that "man was once contained in a little tree shrew, but man is gone." The corollary would raise the question as to what may lie hidden in the human psyche awaiting the opportunity to come out and be "gone" in the fullness of time. Perhaps there lies the "son of man," man's successor, "Homo spiritus." And beyond that, is it not written in the gospels, "I said ye are gods," (John 10:34) "Ye shall see greater things than these." (John 1:50). If Anthropos is the ideal of man, what would the ideal of the man and woman of the future look and be like? The query is beyond our capacity to perceive or to imagine.

Behold, The Man

We come now to the man, Jesus. I indicated in the Introduction that I take the position that Jesus was a human being, not half man, half god, or both at the same time. So important is the question we are raising within the context of evolution that Teilhard's dictum, "henceforth all lines must follow that curve," must now be applied to the lines of a viable Christology. It, too, must follow that curve. Any theology which follows this counsel must be clear at this point.

On my desk I have my favorite icon, a painting, that is a reproduction of a portrait of Jesus by Rembrandt. The background story is interesting. Walking on the sidewalk in Amsterdam, Rembrandt chanced to pass a peasant Jew. Instantly he saw in the countenance of this man an image of Jesus and succeeded in persuading him to come and pose for him. This portrait is the result. It appeals to me more deeply than any I have seen by other artists as a representation of Jesus. In the portrait there is great sadness in his eyes and they seem to be imploring of the viewer, as Jesus did of Peter: "Who do you say that I am?" The lips are parted and the words seem to come forth from him. There is a tenderness in the expression that fulfills Israel's prophesy that the Messiah would be a man of sorrows and acquainted with grief. While it is the most moving and sorrowful of the portraits I know, it is the most earthly as well. Perhaps one should also add the most "hominized," a word coined by Teilhard. I suspect that the portrait is "to the life" a good portrait of that particular peasant Jew. Actually Rembrandt did two portraits of this same man, but I much prefer this one. The original hangs in the Fogg Art Gallery in Cambridge, Massachusetts. It is the humanity that comes out in this portrait. When I look at it for any length of time I, myself, feel addressed by it—"Who do you say that I am?"

The numinous figure of Jesus has dominated the religious life of the Western hemisphere, but it has been pushed down into the unconscious of increasing numbers of Christians since the age of science rose in the eighteenth century. When Jesus is put out of mind as no longer being relevant, he becomes an archetypal figure and takes up his home in the unconscious from which at odd moments he surfaces, making an impact on a given situation.

A few years ago some theologians got together agreeing to the bold claim that "God is dead." This is not a viable myth to live by. I think it is a more tenable thesis to hold that the Christ myth, as it has historically been conceived, is dead for many. It was all right to say that some images of God, as they have been shaped by the Christian Church over the centuries, are "dead" in terms of valid myths of meaning today. But that God is dead, however, cannot be so. If God is dead then there is no point in working on any new Christian or universal myth. Once the prevailing image was that of the sacrificial lamb. Then it was the idea of a cosmic courtroom. Mankind is in the docket. The prisoners are found guilty, but there is no sentence that fits the enormity of the crime. Jesus offers himself, though sinless, as a substitute prisoner, and is found guilty and condemned to death. In this way it could be a substitutionary sacrifice. Some have thought it to be an example to lead the way so that others might be motivated to go and do likewise.

In all these ways, the implication was that Jesus was the awaited Messiah. These images are of a superhuman man, a son of man. The early struggles to answer the query, "Who do you say that I am?" were clearly on the side of divinity. The early councils of the Church succeeded in a verdict to be accepted: Jesus was both man and god, the only son of God, and tempted in all respects, but without sin. "Very God of Very God, begotten not made, being of one substance with the Father," it was nevertheless understood that Jesus was like no other man, that the outer form was something like a mask, disguising the divinity within. There were, of course, some who took the alternative position, that Jesus was perfect man. But in the course of time they were much in the minority.

In a world believing in magic, in which all the major religions emphasized the supernatural, this was not surprising. Indeed it was a world in which the more supernatural the accompanying events were, the better. So the Church opted for an actual growth in miraculous events and god-like behavior of the central figures. This was inevitable. But the Church managed to always have a full spectrum ranging from those who clung to the divine to those who stressed the humanity of Jesus. The tendency of the Church as an institution has been to give more encouragement to the emphasis on the numinous. But in a period dominated by science, in a heroic effort to keep their world one, there have been increasing numbers who have risked charges of heresy in order to maintain mental integrity.

Many of those who have left the Church altogether, and others who have stayed and borne the condemnation and judgment of their fellows because they want to save the Church from the charge of being antiquarian, have increasingly insisted that they be allowed to express their faith in metaphor. I believe that Joseph Campbell has done the Church immeasurable good by interpreting the value of myth and metaphor in his book, *The Power of Myth*. He did a televised series of interviews with Bill Moyers first and later these interviews were transcribed and published as a book. The enormous response, both to the televised interviews and to the book, is an indication that many people are hungry for the opportunity to express their faith in metaphors, rather than be grilled as to their literal beliefs in the form of a creed. Dogmatism is driving many away from the churches and rarely do they find their way back or find groups with whom they may share their beliefs without perjuring their immortal souls.

These people need help to develop the capacity to shape their very own myth of meaning by which to live. They need to be able to articulate it in their own way in solitude and in the company of others without shame and with candor. More than this, they need to think their way through to their own myth of meaning in order to assist the natural forces of instinct in ''getting it together,'' thereby helping the quest of the soul toward the achievement of individuation by way of a mature and healthy religion. The purpose of this quest is to relate more intricately to the world and the universe, and at the same time to bring together a holy synthesis between the conscious and the unconscious. Jung makes a strong case for this work of integration between the conscious and the unconscious on the grounds that growth in consciousness is what the whole process of raised consciousness through further evolution is all about. Jung says that ''the unconscious is the only *accessible* source of religious experience.''

We may begin looking now for material to be incorporated in this myth which, we say again, is to be our very own. It may come from many sources and authors. Inevitably we stand on the shoulders of many here, but the responsibility for balance, credibility, and inspiration in the end is our own. It would be helpful if we could have a Jungian analysis somewhere along the long road, but we can do without it. Friends (Quakers) have developed a process that they call gathering a ''Clearness Committee'' of their own choosing, with whom they meet regularly. It is not the purpose of this committee to answer any burning questions, but rather to raise questions for the seeker to ponder and consider in further wrestling in solitude. Presumably, if the process is working well, there will arise from the unconscious, in the solitary depths of one or more present, another aspect of the problem. This thought or revelation—and it can come to that—can be enormously relevant. It can be so discerning as to inherently offer an answer to the problem under consideration. Some way or another the gathering of the group has so constellated the problem that it has put everything in a new light, interrelating it to other things in such a way as to point to a new set of priorities—a new context that allows for a new possible answer.

The other major resource in resolving the central issue is the practice of contemplative prayer in which the attainment of the darkness, the void, the vastness, and the nothingness can be helpful because the inner posture of the psyche can open up new possibilities for consideration. Then there comes a time of emptiness in which, if one does not press, "Way may open," as Friends say.

The revelation emerging from contemplative prayer is to be granted the benefit of quiet consideration because it is like hearing "the still small voice" of authority. For example, if we wish to shape a personal myth to live by, we must open our hearts and minds so as to see everything in a new light.

Let us see how this works. We want to respond to Jesus' query, "Who do you say that I am?" Surely this is a weighty question. If I am a person whose needs must resolve this first, then I work with it in connection with my own unconscious in terms of watching my dreams and fantasies. I am aware that my answer must be compatible with my myth of meaning. They must cooperate and ultimately agree if they are to serve one master. In my own case, the final answer that will serve me best is one that must conform to certain prerequisites, namely an evolutionary context and the findings of the scientific community exploring from their perspective related or relevant areas of research. I have heard and received for myself the counsel given Teilhard by his novice master. When there is conflict between scientific fact (previously repeated experimentation) and the dogma of the Church, science must be awarded the higher priority. Truth is one. I must keep my right hand well informed as to what my left hand is up to. Teilhard put it this way when he was in process of shaping his myth of meaning.

It is by this faith that I live and it is to this faith, I feel, that at the moment of death, mastering all doubts, I shall surrender my Self. I surrender myself to this undefined faith in a single and infallible world, wherever it may lead me.

It is a good thing that he makes this confession concerning his own quest in search of a myth of meaning. It reflects the intellectual quest, the clarity of finding, and the criterion in his search for truth. Here we see how faithfulness to this position led him "to follow the lines passed by evolution until they reached their maximum coherence." But this is further supported by a recurring mystical experience which is a response of the heart.

Throughout my life, by means of my life, the world has little by little caught fire in my sight until, aflame all around me, it has become almost completely luminous from within—Such has been my experience in contact with the earth—the diaphany of the divine at the heart of a universe on fire . . . Christ, His heart; a fire; capable of penetrating everywhere and gradually spreading everywhere.

Albert Schweitzer, in his mystical experience on the Lambaréné River, heard the magic words that constituted his comfort thereafter: "reverence for life." Teilhard's experience went beyond Schweitzer's. It was as if the voice said that he was to maintain "a reverence for matter," inclusive of life. While his two worlds, the world and his faith, were converging to make one as "two eyes make one in sight," his "inner world" was striving to move toward individuation.

Increasingly he saw Jesus as the evolving man, the Point Omega, and Christogenesis as the counterpart of cosmogenesis in the evolution of man and woman.

One of the points of my critique of Teilhard is that I feel he did not go far enough in his re-mythologizing of the Christ figure. For Teilhard, in a very real sense Christ *was* God, but in a different sense in which God is in all of us. For Teilhard, Jesus was God incarnate. In this day, when Douglas Steere has applied his beautiful phrase "mutual irradiation" to the impact living religions are having on each other, it seems the right time for Christians to abandon forever, but with grace, all the theological claims of exclusiveness that come between us and what we have in common with others, particularly the practice of contemplative prayer and meditation. Teilhard's basic theological structure—his mysticism—does not need an exclusive divinity for Jesus. There is that of God in every man and woman.

Jesus differs from other men and women, not in kind, but in degree. We are all sons and daughters of the living God.

Jung in *The Undiscovered Self* holds that the Church did Jesus a disservice by stressing the imitation of Christ. If one wants to be a faithful disciple of Jesus then one must strive to be as much one's self as Jesus became himself. Individuation is the way forward, not imitation.

It is the study of evolution that enables us to respond to Jesus' query in a new way, compatible with the fresh revelation—the discovery of the process of continuing creation through evolution. When I try to respond to Jesus' query, I have to see him in an evolutionary context and then I have to say that he is fully man. He is more "hominized" than other men and women, and as I have said, more highly evolved than others. He is not differently endowed, but rather more so in certain respects. Paleontologists have a word for this, "sport." In this context it is used to designate a mutation, a breakthrough, a sport. Jesus is a sport (a new metaphor). He is a second Adam, a son of man, man's successor, perhaps the first born among many brothers and sisters, perhaps the first born among the successors to man, "Homo spiritus." To represent the archetypal pattern of higher consciousness is divinity enough for me. In the evolutionary context, it is a tremendous achievement to draw other men and women into the direction they are to follow. That is why we are so drawn to reverence him. That which is incipient in us is already realized in him.

As we have said before, the Christian myth is most prodigiously condensed in its articulation in John 3:16. "God so loved the world that he gave his only begotten son to the end that all that believe in him should not perish but have everlasting life."

In shaping my own myth of meaning I should have to put it this way: God so loved the world that he implanted deeply and darkly in matter itself, the seed which would one day in the fullness of time, by continuing creation through evolution, produce the Christ-life in one Jesus of Nazareth, thereby releasing the Christ seed in other men and women to their soul's salvation and fulfillment.

Far from detracting from the stature of Jesus, this new perspective on him from the evolutionary point of view enhances rather than diminishes him. If he was a man then he is to be judged by the same standards as other men. If he was not a man, but God, the examples he set were something that place no moral injunction upon me. If he were God, then I cannot be judged for failures as a human being. I can have more clarity about what is expected of me. He did this and accomplished that. But it is one thing if he were God, yet quite another if he were man. If God, I might plead with him to intercede for me, to instruct me by urging moral direction at this point or that. But if he be God in any sense, I can only beg mercy of him while doing nothing myself. The whole ethical relationship takes on a new light if he were fully man. We shall be saved by a very different relationship, that of the example he sets, if we have the courage to follow.

If he be God indeed, then I need to plead for forgiveness and to receive the gift until I need to return for more. If he be fully man, I am challenged by his witnessing and I hear the words "Go and do thou likewise." I relate differently according to whether he be man or God. If God, I intercede and feel heard. If man, I am moved, inspired, and find I am motivated to do better. He did all this and was yet a man? And I am a man and could perhaps perform comparable miracles? I am motivated to do better. I grow in self-reliance and ponder the meaning of his astounding words: "Greater things than this will ye do."

Whatever conclusion we come to, it is important to follow through on how it affects not only this relationship but all others in the community of faith.

We can see at once that we must deal with the question of placing the historical figure of Jesus in an evolutionary context. We have already alluded to the importance of Jesus from the point of view of evolution. If we have pondered whether he may be the breakthrough, the crucial mutation, then we may move forward in discerning the implication of this breakthrough. No laws of nature are disturbed. Consistency can be preserved. It is a dependable universe, indeed an infallible one. There will be no anticipation of God's setting aside the rules under which God normally operates for this particular event. There will no longer be the natural and the supernatural, two worlds. It will at all times be one world, under the direction of one God. And the creative resources and the way things operate at a given time will be constant. One may "depend upon the world, the values, the infallibility, the goodness of the world." No empty tomb is needed, indeed no resurrection validated by an empty tomb is needed. It will no longer be necessary to set aside natural law. "Way will open" in the fullness of time, but without the suspension of nature's normal way of performing.

The Values of Evolution

What are the values of the process of evolution? Thomas Berry, student of Teilhard, proposes that we can observe three. The first value is differentiation. Evolution, in the operation of its creative function, favors differentiation. This principle accounts for all mutations. Observe the tree of life and one will realize that the very branches which make the tree a tree are a demonstration of this passion for differentiation. C. G. Jung has a phrase for its operation in the human sphere: the law of individuation.

The second value nature has adopted is the principle of interiority. As a particular line of advance goes forward and the level of consciousness progresses, there is always an increase of interiority. Teilhard had observed that there exists a "within" to everything. It grows as the neurological system develops. The "within" contains the DNA of the particular individual which in turn contains the coding for the development of that individual. On the human level this "within" develops as our interior prayer life deepens. Thus, there is a correlation between contemplation and a focus on the depths of the unconscious as a chosen dwelling place for God.

The third value is communion. Nature, the creative process of evolution, calls for more profound interpenetrating communion as higher consciousness is realized. One can see when, on the human level the qualities of differentiation and interiority are nurtured, there is an opportunity for deeper communion. The more advanced the individuation and interiority, the more profound the potential communion. And the richer the communion, the higher the consciousness ascends.

One may see these three values at work in the psyche and therefore better understand the way evolution encourages the quest of individuation. Within the human psyche there lies the latent potential of further evolution of Homo sapiens, an evolution fostered by contemplative prayer and the richness the quest of individuation affords. Enhanced by differentiation and interiority, one experiences the line of advance of evolution and senses with Paul the joy of being a creator with God in the process of communion. The value of a human being grows with the deliberate cultivation of these evolutionary values. The query "What is man that thou art mindful of him?" wins for man and woman a new reputation. The old concept of Anthropos and the associations with that archetype must be allowed to evolve in the present context.

The way we see Jesus affects our current response to his query. Certainly we have a different perspective as a result of our discovery of the fact of evolution.

I must complete my answer. I believe Jesus to be a Jewish mystic, prophet, leader, healer. He is not the Son of God in any exclusive sense. The nature of his relationship to one he called Father, his God, governed by love, obedience, and a passion to pursue an appointed mission, has surpassed that of any other contemplative man or woman of his time. Every man and woman of any time or place entertains in the unconscious a notion of what a perfect human being would be like. Jesus was no exception to the general rule. In him it took the form of a mystical experience of unity with God—an experience he wanted for all men and women henceforth. We shall now consider the mystical or contemplative faculty as the emerging direction of our continuing evolutionary development.

CHAPTER THREE

The Development of the Mystical Faculty

Our personal myth of meaning must have a positive attitude toward mysticism. The individual will want to work out a position regarding this basic element in all true religion. Ever since religious institutions began to notice distinctive types of religious piety, there has been a good deal of wariness in the attitude of those in power toward what has been called mysticism since the third century. The suspicion had to do with an important issue, the ultimate source of authority. The vast majority placed their confidence in the authority of a book, in an institutional hierarchy, in a general convention or council.

On the other hand, the mystics characteristically put their confidence in the God who dwells within, God immanent. One drawing up his or her personal myth of meaning will need to learn in some depth what the mystical approach to religious experience has been and still is. There has been a mystical element in all the living religions. It has been said that the mystics do not disagree. The organizational structures are different and would find their differences a block to agreement on important issues. Those who take a fundamentalist stand regarding scripture periodically have even larger and more intensive disagreements with each other. But since mysticism is always an individual experience, mystics are inclined to support one another in their differences. The Church generally has not been so generous. Indeed she has excommunicated many of her mystics. I like to refer to the ''apostolic succession'' of Christian mystics. There is also the apostolic succession of all mystics inclusive of all religions.

What Is Mysticism?

There is a no more abused word in the religious vocabulary than mysticism. To call one a mystic can, in a given context, be either derogatory or complimentary. It can be intended as an insulting remark or a high tribute. We shall need to agree as to its connotations—else we shall contribute to the general confusion.

The word mysticism was first introduced by the so-called "Mystery Religions" at the time of early Christianity. The word had a distinctive purpose. These religions encouraged the sense of mystery and secrecy, partly because they needed protection from possible persecution. While these religions were autonomous, they had a good deal of influence upon other religions and vice versa. St. Augustine was profoundly influenced by the early mystics and in turn contributed to the planting of the mystical seed that has subsequently borne enormous fruit within and outside the Church.

But let us pause to reflect upon the meaning of mysticism. It is easier to say what it is not than what it is. In the East they are fond of saying "not this, not that," "neti neti." It has also been frequently said: "He who knows what it is doesn't say, while he who says what it is doesn't know." There is a good deal of gentle humor as well as truth in this. But partly because of these statements, which sometimes have a precautionary intent, the curiosity of those who feel drawn to the mystical way flourished and at least for a season there was a vigorous witness. The Middle Ages encouraged the mystical movement. Rufus Jones designated the fourteenth century as "The Flowering of Mysticism." One thinks especially of Meister Eckhart and others of that period. The word took on additional associations and many different definitions were offered.

Happily, during the last century, there has been considerable research into the meaning and value of mysticism. Engaged in this work were Evelyn Underhill, E. Herman, Rufus Jones, Dean Inge, Walter Stace, Rudolph Otto, Baron von Hugel, and others.

What is so extraordinary about these interpreters of mysticism is that none of them claimed to be mystics. Yet all aspired to study the mystic way. In their approach to the research, they worked independently and therefore did not influence one another, with one exception. Baron von Hugel undoubtedly influenced Evelyn Underhill, for whom he served as spiritual guide for a number of years. While they arrived at their conclusions independently, there was an enormous degree of corroboration in their findings. None of them claimed to be a mystic. On the contrary, most of them would have concurred with Walter Stace of Princeton. I asked him directly if he was a mystic. "Oh no," he said, "I'm not a mystic. I know where the sacred mountain is, but, alas, I have not climbed it." All of these researchers knew vicariously the mountain he referred to. They were modest about any claims to have scaled it, but all agreed that it was the heart of all true religion.

As I have said, it is easier to know what mysticism is not than what it is. They all agreed that mysticism and the mystical way is not the same as the psychic way. Psychic experience is not the same as mystical experience. There are various forms of psychic experience. Psychic experiences can relate to the satanic or the occult and include clairvoyance and spiritualism which purport to get in touch with departed spirits. Hearing voices and seeing visions are psychic phenomena. Channeling is a psychic experience just as much as some of the phenomena of the charismatic churches. The Holy Spirit is at work in such a group. The authenticity is self-evident.

But there are important differences between psychic and mystical experiences. In mystical experiences there is a built-in moral imperative based on love that is given and received, which seems wanting in the psychic equivalent. Psychic gifts can be put to evil use. The same person can have different experiences, mystical and psychic, at different times. Jesus could have both kinds of experience. Clairvoyantly perceiving Matthew at the receipt of Customs and the mystical baptismal experience of Jesus were not the same kind of experience.

There are three criteria that can be used in discerning the mystical experience. The first is that of being loved. Not of loving initially, but of being loved. William Johnston in his book, *The Inner Eye of Love*, makes very clear the primacy of this initial experience. The love that is experienced is unconditional, without restrictions or reservations. It transcends human love. In every case it comes by surprise and is different from every other experience that this particular person has had, even of the same mystical love.

The second characteristic is the experience of an identification with an object. The person is surprised to discover that he or she indwells the other, and vice versa. It is a singular sense of being in that other and that other being in oneself. It may be an object in nature, as with Wordsworth. It is as if that other wants to impart something. So, in "Intimations of Immortality" Wordsworth writes:

> There's a tree, of many, one
> A single field which I have looked upon.

There is a sense of interpenetration and an infusion of a presence. Again, Wordsworth, in another poem:

> And I have felt
> A presence that disturbs me with the joy
> Of elevated thoughts; a sense sublime
> Of something far more deeply interfused,
> Whose dwelling is the light of setting suns
> And the round ocean and the living air,
> And the blue sky, and in the mind of man;

The visual artist who is also a mystic can depict this presence on canvas. The cypress tree and the green grass remain what they are, cypress tree and grass, but the artist, Van Gogh, has managed to interrelate these in an effective way. It is quite clear that they are dancing to the music of the same drummer. Furthermore, the artist is dancing with them. The pointillist is able to suggest the "something far more deeply interfused" as represented by the dots to which everything can be reduced.

Finally, the friends of the person who has the mystical experience note that he or she is transformed, at least for the present. They remark that somehow he or she has it together. There is a new coherence in his or her personality. He or she is a more loving person. It may be that he or she has become a happier person. Perhaps he or she has become a channel for love. It may be that the love seems to come through the person from afar. It may be that the love of God is channeled through him or her.

Some are openly offended by the way others have become mystics, while they are unable for some reason to "make the grade." Still others are envious but feel it is a matter of genes and they have not been destined to become mystics. But Meister Eckhart, whom Rufus Jones called the peak of the range in the flowering of mysticism in the fourteenth century, was fond of saying, "The mystic is not a special kind of person. Every person is a special kind of mystic"—a much more hopeful statement.

Eckhart, a great Dominican preacher, has a series of sermons in which the mystical is set forth in almost a jubilant way. There is a light-heartedness that is delightful. He is almost debonair about the current kingdom on earth and the ease with which one may enter. It is winsome and charming. One of these sermons is entitled "The

Aristocrat." It helps to know the background.

Eckhart's father had been the chief steward in the house of a nobleman or aristocrat. It is somewhat daunting to think of his father producing a son like Eckhart, and then of Eckhart, the son, becoming a Dominican friar. What is still more daunting is to realize that he was valiantly making use of this metaphor, "aristocrat." Undoubtedly his father found being a servant a demeaning task. And his son must have chafed under this confinement. But now the son is using the word in a totally different context. He is urging his congregation to be aristocrats in a different way. They are to become aristocrats in the only aristocracy that ultimately matters, the aristocracy of the spirit. They are, furthermore, to take their place in the apostolic succession of mystics.

On Becoming a Mystic for the Sake of the World

There was a time when most of those on this quest to become a contemplative did so for their own sakes, for the salvation of their own souls. One of the encouraging developments in recent decades is that there are many now who undertake the arduous journey, not so much for their own sakes, as for the sake of the world. It is a sorry world we live in. It is a world in which many current species are in danger of extinction. And now Homo sapiens is becoming, if it is not already, an endangered species. Paleontologists tell us that the basis of extinction, the reason it takes place, is that the animal has become over-specialized to the extent that it cannot adjust to the changing environment in which it lives. The saber-toothed tiger did very well until the fang got so large it reduced its usefulness and was actually in the way. The environment changed and the tooth that had been so successful in getting food now become a handicap in gathering the daily supply. Some birds became so heavy that their very weight put an intolerable burden on the wings and they became extinct.

The same syndrome is now affecting the human race. We are over-specializing in a number of ways. We have learned how to prolong life, but have not willed birth control. We consume extravagantly, but we do not conserve our resources. No animal has ever so fouled its nest as the human animal. We apply our wonderful gift of creating technology to specializing in building the implements of destruction. Certain products continue to be produced despite their danger to our health. We destroy appealing environments for the sake of building homes or commercial ventures of one kind or another. Our promotion of what ironically is called real estate is in utter disregard of life and has been at the price of the extinction of many species. It is estimated that in another ten years, by the turn of the century, no less than one hundred thousand more species will be destroyed. And when a species has been destroyed and become extinct, no power on earth can ever bring it back. The universe has lost a part of itself, never to be recovered.

What man has done and is doing to the good earth is devastating. In *The Dream of the Earth*, Thomas Berry spells out for us the actual diminishments the earth has suffered already, and what exactly is happening to the earth right now. This book, published by the Sierra Club, is the first in a series to be called Nature Library.

Amid all the destruction of the earth, now and again one hears of local concerns to save species that are endangered. Such solitary efforts restore our hope. I think of the woman in Texas who gathers up young sea turtles and takes them to inland waterways during the season when thousands would otherwise be lost on beaches before they reach a certain degree of maturity. These valiant efforts to save species, and many others like them, give us hope and inspiration. But we must act with all the energy we can summon if our efforts are to count. When one's hope is dampened, this kind of dedicated action is very encouraging.

One of the special blessings bestowed on humankind is sentience. It enables us to assess our predicament and to think our way through our problem. Man and woman are the first creatures on earth who know what the impending disaster would mean. We are the only creatures who can work with active imagination to counterbalance the danger and alter the consciousness, enabling a checking of the pace with which the disaster is approaching. If we are willing to make sacrifices, not only can we slow the pace of deterioration, but perhaps even reverse the trend with positive programs that may restore or replace what has been lost. Something has begun to change already. It is as though a trumpet of arousal has blown and men and women are responding everywhere. It is another blessing that we have the scientific knowledge to know what to do, if we would save ourselves.

We need at once to enlarge our research programs, recalling Teilhard's insight that research is a form of adoration. In this instance research is also communion with the rest of nature over a shared interest in a renewal of the earth. We have a resource that no other animal on this tree of life has been accorded: the capacity to reflect and to experiment consciously. We can be proud of what we have already done to save ourselves. But the number of persons, both informed and presently engaged in doing something about it, is pitiably small. Yet the field of potential is ripe to the harvest.

An enormous job awaits those educated among us to spread the word to those who are not yet informed. This is the first task. The next task, following the dissemination of knowledge, is that of organizing the special projects under the direction of our ablest scientists and making the restoration of the planet priority number one. I conceive this being overseen by the United Nations after the crucial step of appointing the best scientists available and bringing them together with leaders of industry and management. Our new symbol is the picture of our beautiful planet, taken from the moon, 250,000 miles out.

It has been said that when adversaries are suddenly confronted by a third, they are automatically converted into allies. There is much hope that the former enemy of the United States, the Soviet Union, might become a real ally ready to stand with us against a common enemy, the progressive deterioration of the planet earth. After all, if our planet should become bereft of life, every other concern to which men and women give their energy in abundance would have to be abandoned. Therefore, this concern must be number one. If the common concern could bring us together and evoke a new bonding, then a new age would be ushered in—an age in which we would be united in the politics of ecology. Imagine if the budgets of defense in both Russia and the United States could become one international program to save the earth?

Toward a New Cosmic Mysticism

This world of ours is the home and base of raised consciousness and sentience. We do not know whether the vast universe contains, anywhere else, the life that has until now flourished on the earth. There is, therefore, an enormous weight of responsibility resting upon us. What if there were no other creatures in the universe with sentience? We have been given the responsibility of preserving all other forms of life that contribute to the life community. We need to know about mysticism and why we believe it could save the earth. As we have seen, mysticism is the experience that all this vast creation is indwelt by God. God is immanent as well as transcendent, not only in man and woman, but at the heart of all things. He or she is "the diaphany of the divine at the heart of matter" itself. When Teilhard was challenged for what his interrogators thought to be pantheism, which they could have excommunicated him for, Teilhard carefully explained that he had never said that God and matter were one, but that God was at the heart of matter and that he had perceived God as a luminescence from within. Then he proceeded to give this faith a name: "panentheism," God in matter. This seemed to satisfy his interrogators in the Vatican. This is not to identify God with matter but to see God within matter. Just as Francis had found God in all creatures, Teilhard found God in all things and answered to that of God in all things.

Prayer to the God Within

Prayer to the transcendent God, who remains transcendent, is still important. But the same God is also immanent. One addresses that transcendent God in meditative prayer where words are used and thoughts and feelings are expressed in a rational way. These prayers include praise, thanksgiving, confession, intercession, and petition. These are the classic forms of meditative prayer. They give expression to the external relationship between the penitent in communion with the transcendent God. One might say that they are all responses to that of God in the universe.

But there is also God immanent, God within. How is God immanent addressed in prayer? The mystics hold that the appropriate form of prayer to God within is contemplative prayer, the prayer of silence, of adoration in silence. One must quiet the body by whatever means the person praying finds congenial, perhaps some form of yoga. A biblical phrase or mantra may serve to quiet the mind, so much that it may abandon rational thought, ultimately even "imaging," and the constant stream of consciousness. Now the psyche can turn in confidence to that altered state of consciousness that the mystics of all the living religions describe by the same metaphors: nothingness, emptiness, the void, darkness. We are reminded by the Old Testament that the God of Israel chose to dwell in "thick darkness." In the light of the perceptions of depth psychology, this thick darkness may be seen as the unconscious.

In this thick darkness also dwell the demonic impulses, the shadow side of God. It is necessary to learn how to discern God's will in the unconscious and to differentiate God from the darkness in which he or she has determined to live. Wait in trust. Wait in penitence. Wait in expectation of some form of transformation. Wait in emptiness, integrity, and hopefulness. Since, as Jung says, the archetype of the self and the archetype of the Self, God within, are ultimately indistinguishable, wait in patience for the God within to speak through the still, small voice. Wait for God in the depths of one's own being to irradiate the soul, while one is patient that the process may go forward. Intermediate between meditative prayer and contemplation is the prayer of active imagination. Wait while the body and spirit are consciously plugged into the golden thread of evolution. Here it helps to feel and see where one has come from on this planet and where one may be tending toward in the still evolving psyche.

One with active imagination may rehearse the steps by which these successive transformations have taken place. It is a process of imagining an infinite regression back in time to stardust and the void, and then re-entry from the void to stardust to subatomic particles to the first cells to the tree of life forward, along the path of complexity consciousness to, perhaps, "Homo spiritus." If we are right in discerning that rising-consciousness has been the propulsive energy that has taken us forward on the tree of life, then one offers one's whole psyche to cooperate with this further evolution. One accepts the inward shaping of our little vessel by the two hands of the divine potter, one within the psyche and the other pressing from outside, in order to keep the restless body on its evolutionary way. Probably from now on the body will not change much, but there was a time when small changes in the nervous system and the size of the cranial cavity were effecting enormous change in the brain's development. Research on the structure and function of the brain within and across species made it evident that centimeters of space had to open up before certain capacities of the brain could be accommodated.

In human evolution, two changes in the body were critically important: the growth and shape of the brain and the change in the hands that had once been furry paws. The thumb grew into juxtaposition with every finger, enabling the hand to hold implements and tools, to thrust spears and other weapons, to consciously invent things as labor-saving devices, and to pursue manifold forms of art. Now it is possible to study the species and determine what would assist evolution to move in the direction it wants to go. If one believes that the goal is ever higher levels of consciousness, then cooperation and co-creation can go forward in prayer. Movement along this curved line can be aided by long periods of adoration. We come ever closer to that which we adore. This is why the prayer of adoration is so relevant when applied to conscious cooperation with creation through evolution. For the first time in the long history of evolution, there is an animal who can consciously participate in the operation of transformation, within limits.

Toward a New Spirituality of the Earth

The myth of cosmogenesis is supported by the myth of purposive evolution. The cosmos is still being born. We can almost watch it taking place. Prayer is the most effective means of cooperation. Our motivation is the mystical sense of identification, the realization that all the creatures on the tree of life are related to us far enough back and deep enough down. There are some people who are gifted with the capacity to communicate with animals, but all of us, in varying degrees, are able to relate much more profoundly than we give ourselves credit for. One has only to read the books of Loren Eiseley to see how effortless the process can be. He managed to write quite a few books before his untimely death. The manner in which he enters into playful communication with the foxes and courts a stork at the zoo, invites us to participate in this innocent and joyous occupation and recreation.

The religion of the immediate future, in order to be relevant to the crisis of our loss of engagement with the earth, has to include knowledge of and familiarity with other creatures. A mystical identification with other creatures may protect them from the possible extinction that might otherwise be their lot.

What is needed is a spirituality of the earth, an ''earth mysticism.'' Not a spirituality directed to the earth, but a spirituality *of* the earth. I mean this in the sense of evolving naturally from the earth, the earth's own spirituality, and arising out of the earth as we have arisen out of the earth. This is a very important element in our personal myth of meaning. To be viable, it must further a profound relationship to the earth. We have to create liturgies, pageantry, and ceremonies to enable a new earth mysticism to begin to form. What a creative pursuit this will be for many when we begin to see it unfold!

The earth has contained as a seed from the time it was born the substance out of which we emerged in the fullness of time. Every substance that has combined with other substances to form our bodies and psyche was derived from the earth. In the committal service in the Book of Common Prayer there is the familiar phrase "earth to earth, ashes to ashes, dust to dust." We might add "consciousness to consciousness."

Until the process of evolution was discovered by Charles Darwin we were unaware of how profoundly true this is. When the body is put into the earth there is a veritable homecoming. We are earthlings. The earth is in every particle of our bodies. Insofar as men and women pray, it is the earth at prayer. Insofar as we deepen our knowledge and love of the earth, we aid in creating with the earth her own distinctive spirituality. Insofar as men and women experience ecstasy, the earth experiences ecstasy for the first time. Would God we could undo what we have done to the earth!

Alas, it is not possible to set back the hands of the earth clock a few million years and have a new start! How different it would be. Yes, perchance, but until the hearts of men and women change, any effort of ours will not be so different. What we need to do is to band together as swiftly as possible and, as Thomas Berry has put it, "reinhabit the earth," this time honoring our "mother" at every turn. There are still many things one can do in the way of recycling, preserving, and conserving, and many research possibilities. Quakers on the West Coast have initiated and organized a movement called "Friends of the Earth" which, in turn, has produced a pamphlet entitled "Walking Gently on the Earth," an inspired metaphor which is being put to good service, judged by the response it is winning from many individuals and small groups. It brings together a compendium of ideas one can do or small groups can do to make public witness.

This concern among Friends, along with other concerns, has bid fair to join the historic testimonies of Friends. It is important to keep track of the expanding list of what one can do. Moreover, there has been so much response from Friends that the organization, supported by mature reflection and experienced activists, could accomplish much by welding a larger group together. We need to engage in "network building" in order that sheer numbers in the course of time could make a formidable impression in the States and elsewhere. Thomas Berry in his book, *The Dream of the Earth*, uses another metaphor: "reenchantment with the earth." We have commended this book already. It is well, however, to do so again here that the suggestion may not be forgotten.

The United Nations in 1984 adopted a wonderful *Bill of Rights for Nature*. This is an extraordinary document, unique in human history. It reflects deep concern and gives it sound articulation. It is an inclusive "call to arms" that any good pacifist would find congenial. The concern for the earth and a new earth/human relationship is proving contagious, and will continue to inspire many individuals and groups. One group guides another and whoever lit the first candle becomes magnified by the natural processes of mutual irradiation. Little circles are springing up all over the world.

But the greatest gift by individuals to the overall movement is the recollection or inward gathering that must take place on the inward journey. Faithfulness in meditation and contemplation is the first priority. If we were to become contemplatives (mystics) right now, we would make our maximum contribution to the earth/human relationship that is so crucial to the renewal of the earth.

The restoration of the earth follows learning from the earth and discovering what the earth is asking of us in support of her own spirituality. This comes first. Not that other concerns are to be abandoned. Many of them are to be steadily supported. But the first claim on our energy and on raised consciousness is the tender loving care we must bestow on the earth. The earth, the very cosmos, is awaiting the development of more contemplatives who have become capable of mystical communion with the earth. Once it was enough that a few solitary souls sought to become contemplatives for their soul's sake. Now there are indications that many are drawn to this solitary quest for the sake of the world. DeCaussade would call this process "Abandonment to Divine Providence" with reference to the earth, its needs, and its revelation of God within.

Worshipping the God of the Ahead

Finally, Teilhard makes another distinction—this time between the God of the Above and the God of the Ahead. The God of the Above is the God Transcendent, the creator and sustainer of the universe, the great Holy One. And the God of the Ahead is the God of evolution. This is the God made known in every mutation and transformation, and in the creation of new species to be assimilated into the life community on this earth. The God of the Ahead is the mysterious entity who or which attracts and then draws forward in union whatever is needed for the realization of the next phase of growth toward raised consciousness. Meanwhile, silently and secretly, the magnetic pull of this God of the Ahead is aided by the push of the God within. Together they hold, gather, and draw forward continuing creation toward an unknown denoument in the fullness of time, the eschatological event, the Point Omega.

It is hard for me to follow Teilhard here. I do not understand how we can confidently predict any end for evolution. I am wondering whether Teilhard had fallen victim to his own grounding in an eschatology inherited from his Judaeo-Christian background. He speaks of a cosmogenesis and a Christogenesis which are on convergent courses. But I find it difficult to see, within its own structure, any end to evolution that does not also involve the end of the universe. Having spoken out on the issue of the Fall in the Garden of Eden, and being under the surveillance of his superiors, and having tried them to the utmost, I think he had an unconscious need to remain orthodox on the divinity of Jesus, his resurrection, and "point omega," lest he be excommunicated. I think he was tempted to remain silent or at least reticent in this area.

Some of his friends tried to persuade him to leave the Jesuit Order and find a liberal bishop in some diocese who would tolerate his theological ideosyncracies. But, as stated earlier, he looked upon the Society of Jesus as his "divine milieu" and was confident he would never leave it unless driven from it. Furthermore, he had the assurance that his writing in the critical areas of philosophy and theology would ultimately be published through an agreement with Jeanne Mortier. That was enough for him. Did he not say that his writing represented preliminary findings, and that others coming after him would test, correct, and complete his work? There is nothing sacrosanct about his work. His writings constitute one man's hard won findings, one man's personal myth of meaning, one man's vision. It was a magnificent attempt to reconcile science and theology. This effort at integration was much needed and continues in the work of others.

The work is far from completed. Much needs to be done, especially with regard to the doctrines of the Virgin Birth, the Resurrection of the Body, and the Life Everlasting. But Teilhard's myth of meaning is a monumental achievement. It has inspired an uncounted number of theologians to build on the basic foundations of his thought and to shape their own personal myth of meaning anew, following his realization of the need even for our Christology to follow "the curve which all lines must henceforth follow: the curve of evolution.''

Perhaps the greatest contribution made by Teilhard was not so much his theological innovations as his lived mysticism and its expression. It was truly an earth mysticism, which such as what is so desperately needed today. He did, indeed, ''walk gently on the earth'' with reverence, respect, courtesy, and love. I am aware that it is his myth of meaning that has encouraged me to take off on my own quest, and while I part company with him at several important places and do not quite understand him at other places, I fully accept his appraisal of the importance of evolution as a perspective and starting point for shaping one's own personal myth of meaning.

CHAPTER FOUR

The Eternal Feminine

There is no indication that Jesus looked down on women. On the contrary, with Mary as his mother he must have had at the very beginning of his life many reasons to honor and respect women. Women were drawn to him and he to them. He may have been in love with Mary Magdalene. It is certain that he made visits to Mary and Martha's home for comfort and refreshment. He was courteous and sensitive to the woman taken in adultery. He put the Samaritan woman at the well at ease. Further, in some way he must have cultivated the feminine in himself.

Salvadore Dali's painting of the Last Supper, which hangs in the National Gallery of Art in Washington, D.C., has so portrayed the countenance of Jesus that, apart from the other figures in the painting, it could be taken for either man or woman. It has an androgynous quality about it. The eternal feminine had to come into the painting in some way and the artist, in my judgment, depicted it in just the right way for our age. We have been persuaded that the human psyche has both masculine and feminine components. C. G. Jung has made this psychological observation very convincing.

The Masculine and Feminine Components

There are some militant feminists who insist that there are no masculine and feminine qualities—that there are only qualities or characteristics, and whether any one of them dominates in a given man or woman is a matter of chance and culture. I agree that some men have more or stronger so-called feminine characteristics than some women and vice versa. But when we are talking of men in general and women in general, I think that statistically we can determine qualities or characteristics that are more common to women and those that are more developed in men. Moreover, when there are such radical differences physiologically, these differences must be reflected in the psyche as well. It is quite another thing to say that because of this there are some vocations appropriate for males and others appropriate for females. What we have learned is that women can do as well as men, if not better, in a surprising number of vocations that formerly were reserved for men. Their way of doing some things may be different (and this is being studied extensively) but they should not be excluded from any vocation simply on the ground that they are women. And if chosen for a job, they should be paid the same salary for the same job.

A man can be as nurturing as a woman if called to be both father and mother in a case where the child has been deprived of a mother. A woman can be as good a train engineer or truck driver as any man, provided she is strong in those characteristics called for in that occupation. Women in general may be better at working with children in a kindergarten than most men, but some men excel at working with young children. In the latter case, the feminine component is stronger in these men than statistically would be the case for the average man. It was assumed for centuries that men were better qualified as priests. Now most of us know better, but the prejudices and the chauvinism persist.

I like the distinction made by the Jungian analyst, Irene Claremont de Castillejo in her book *Knowing Woman*. She holds that the clearest distinction (again, speaking of averages) is that of the nature of consciousness. Men generally have focused consciousness, whereas most women are coming from a more diffuse awareness. I believe it is sound to draw the distinction from the difference in habitual forms of consciousness. Other distinctions are more or less derived from this base. Many, including Jung and Teilhard, whom we have been taking for our guides at a number of junctures, speak of the feminine as gifted in the relational. If we agree that there are gifts that are characteristically feminine or masculine, we would be inclined to grant that the woman is the more likely to excel in the relational. That profile seems to fall naturally within the feminine sphere in families as well as in corporations.

Jane Hollister Wheelwright of the San Francisco Jung Institute and the Inter-Regional Society of Jungian Analysts, has an interesting comment in her essay, "Old Age and Death." She says,

"I know that archetypal woman is said to be concerned not only with life, but with its opposite, death, as well." In another place she writes, speaking of death:

> I like to think that when I go, I will become part of nature. I know of no more miraculous, fantastic scheme, no more perfect design for life and death, than nature. In nature life and death are equally important. . . . So my fantasy, as of this point anyhow, is to melt into nature when I die: to become part of the trees, part of all vegetation; part of earth and rocks, also animals, birds, even the reptiles and insects or anything else that moves—in short become part of the goddess of nature who, if we would only realize it, could be standing side by side with our Christian God. . . . I may not as yet be honoring sufficiently the huge achievements of consciousness made under the aegis of the Christian God. But as a modern woman, I am more concentrated on establishing in my imagination the guiding force of the female deity before contemplating the male. Modern woman at any age has to anchor herself firmly in the female before she can give due respect to the male, or so I believe.

Jane Wheelwright makes another interesting point on the Feminist Movement:

> In the Feminist Movement we see the revolution of women against the traditional concept of being considered "nothing" in their own right. However, women possibly have failed to appreciate and value their essential female nothingness—their ability to let live, to step aside for the benefit of others. Perhaps they need to recognize, and to tell men, that, like God the Void, they too are divine in their nothingness. (Granted, of course, that they have to assert themselves first as being everything before they can risk extolling their nothingness: "All and nothing" might be the woman's cry.)

The Feminine is the Unitive

In one of his last writings, *The Heart of Matter*, Teilhard concludes with a brief essay entitled "The Feminine, or the Unitive." It begins:

> The living heart of the Tangible is the Flesh. And for Man the Flesh means Woman. Ever since my childhood I had been engaged in the search for the Heart of Matter, and so it was inevitable that sooner or later I should come up against the Feminine.
> As I tell the story in these pages of my inner vision, I would be leaving out an essential element, or atmosphere, if I did not add in conclusion

that from the critical moment when I rejected many of the old molds in which my family life and my religion had formed me and began to wake up and express myself in terms that were really my own, I have experienced no form of self-development without some feminine eye turned on me, some feminine influence at work.

When I say this, you will understand, of course, that I mean simply that general, half-worshipping homage which sprang from the depths of my being and was paid to those women whose warmth and charm have been absorbed drop by drop, into the life blood of my most cherished ideas. . . .

It seems to be indisputable (both logically and factually) that there can be for man—even if he be devoted to the service of a Cause or of a God, and however great that devotion—no road to spiritual maturity or plenitude except through some ''emotional'' influence whose function is to sensitize his understanding and stimulate, at least initially, his capacity for love. Every day supplies more irrefutable evidence that no man at all can dispense with the Feminine, any more than he can dispense with light, or oxygen, or vitamins.

Secondly, however primordial in human psychism the plenifying encounter of the sexes may be, and however essential to its structure, there is nothing to prove (indeed, the opposite is much more true) that we yet have an exact idea of the functioning of this fundamental complementarity or of the best forms in which it can be effected. We have a marriage that is always polarized, socially, toward reproduction, and a religious perfection that is always represented, theologically, in terms of separation, and there can be no doubt but that we lack a third road between the two. I do not mean a middle road, but a higher, a road that is demanded by the revolutionary transformation that has recently been effected in our thought by the transposition of the notion of ''spirit.'' For the spirit that comes from dematerialization, we have seen, we have substituted the spirit that comes from synthesis, Materia Matrix. It is no longer a matter of retreating (by abstinence) from the unfathomable spiritual powers that still lie dormant under the mutual attraction of the sexes, but of conquering them by sublimation. Such, I am ever more convinced, is the hidden essence of Chastity, and such the magnificent task that awaits it.

Both those assertions fall into place and are justified if we look at them from the following point of view.

In my interpretation of Noogenesis I have so far emphasized the phenomenon of individual super-centration, which causes the consciousness of the corpuscular to fold back upon itself and thence rebound in the form of Thought. But now an essential complement to this great cosmic event of Reflection becomes apparent to the informed eye, and it takes the form of what we might call ''the Breakthrough into

Amorization." Even after the flash of illumination in which the individual is suddenly revealed to himself, elementary Man would remain but half complete if he did not come into contact with the other sex and so, under the centric attraction of person to person, explode into flame.

First we have the appearance of a reflective monad, and then, to complete it, the formation of an affective dyad.

And, after that, and only after that (that is, starting from this first spark) all that we have described follows in sequence—the gradual and majestic development of a Neo-cosmic, of an Ultra-human, and of a Pan-Christic . . .

All three not only illuminated in their very roots by Intelligence, but also impregnated throughout their entire mass, as though bonded by a unifying cement, by the Universal Feminine.

Elsewhere, in the essay entitled, "The Evolution of Chastity" Teilhard says, "spirituality falls on the dyad, not the monad." This is a surprising thing for a Jesuit priest to say, but obviously he is speaking straight from the heart. And, to put all this in context, he does conclude the essay with a defense of celibacy as being "a more excellent way," but only when one is genuinely called to it and when one is careful to have access to women as friends and companions. In a creative relationship the universal feminine must always be present because in the mystery of the universal feminine is hidden the divine milieu.

Sexuality and Spirituality

C. G. Jung called attention to the fact that just as there are masculine genes in the genetic makeup of every woman, so there are feminine genes in the DNA and a feminine component in the genetic makeup of every man. He felt it was important that men and women should consciously attempt to cultivate the contrasexual component that abides in all of us. Indeed, the men and women in whom the anima and animus are well integrated stand a better chance of making a good marriage than those in whom this is not the case. Teilhard and Jung are examples of men who consciously cultivated the feminine in themselves. In albums of family pictures one can follow the transformation as the very lines of their countenances reflected the inner development of the feminine.

In the essay from which we have been quoting, Teilhard says:

In short, we often hear sexuality has no significance at all from the moral and religious point of view: you might as well speak of running your digestion on moral principles. So far as his sexual side is concerned, man must no doubt have a care for health, and exercise temperance. A controlled use will give him balance and an added zest for action. But by no stretch of imagination can we agree that physical chastity has anything to do with the spiritual. There is no direct relationship between sanctity and sexuality.

We can no longer picture ourselves as standing apart from the animal kingdom. Remy de Gourmant is indisputably right when he asserts that:

There is no gulf between man and the animals . . . we are animals . . . When we make love . . . we truly do so, to use the theologian's phrase, "more bestiarum" like the beasts. Love is deeply animal.

Teilhard then quotes from Pierre Burney's reference to Jean Rostand.

Whether one likes it or not, whatever ideas one upholds, the whole fabric of human love, with all the animality and the sublimation the word implies, with its frenzy and its self-sacrifice, and with all its lightness of touch, its pathos and its terrors, is yet built upon the minute molecular variations of a new compound of phenanthrene. Does this take all the poetry out of love?

To which Burney replies:

Now Rostand has reached the nadir of materialist reduction but abruptly he reverses the process with this profound saying, "Does this take all the poetry out of love? What if it fills chemistry with poetry?"

Teilhard was profoundly concerned, and wanted to help create a new sex ethic, or rather to remythologize the Christian myth at this point. He writes:

It used to be urged that the natural manifestations of love should be reduced as much as possible. We now see that the real problem is how to harness the energy they represent and transform them. Such will be our new ideal of chastity . . . Rightly speaking, there are no sacred or profane things, no pure or impure; there is only a good direction and a bad direction—the direction of ascent, of amplifying unity, of greatest spiritual effort; and the direction of descent, of constricting egoism, of materializing enjoyment. If these are followed in the direction that leads upward, all creatures are luminous; if grasped in the direction which leads downward, they lose their radiance and become, we might almost say, diabolical. According to the skill with which we set our sails to their breeze, it will either capsize our vessel or send it leaping ahead.

What Teilhard seems to be saying is that spirit extends all the way down in ever more primitive forms into animal sexuality and below into the source of life in matter. But if it is spirit all the way down into animal sexuality and below, the inevitable and irrevocable corollary is that it is sex all the way up into the highest reaches of spirit achieved by humankind and beyond. In our terms sex is the channel through which the ascent of the spirit has primarily taken place in animals, reaching its current peak in the human animal.

The process in which spirit rises through sex is one of sublimation. The marks of the spirit which Paul so effectively identified—love, joy, peace, patience, kindness, goodness, fidelity, gentleness, and self-control—became the standard for the various forms which the sublimation must take if sex in the individual is to be a channel for continued growth in the life of the spirit. What is of extreme importance is the direction in which spirit is moving in the sexual expression of an individual—that is, whether it is moving retrogressively toward more primitive animality or progressively toward more sublimated hominization.

Teilhard then turns to the question of celibacy and physical chastity. He might be expected to remain loyal to his vocational choice, which might be known as his particular divine milieu. I cannot follow his reasoning here. I acknowledge that "the celibate life makes a special witness," but I cannot concede any "absolute superiority" or that some "perfection lies in virginity by nature." Teilhard refers to the heroine of a Russian novel (which he does not name) as expressing the idea that "We shall in the end find another way of loving." A spiritual fecundity will apparently supercede material fecundity. "Union for the sake of the child, but why not union for the sake of the work, for the sake of the idea?" he asks. Then he suggests that sublimation of the flesh is precisely what many men of genius, men who have been true creators, have instinctively found and adopted.

When Teilhard says that "Virginity rests upon chastity as thought upon life," I cannot accept the claim, but I go along with the conclusion:

> It is biologically evident that to gain control of passion and so make it serve spirit must be a condition of progress.

Teilhard saves his most powerful metaphor for the very end of the essay:

> The day will come when, after harnessing the winds, the waves, the tides, and gravity, we shall harness for God the energies of love. And on that day, for the second time in the history of the world, man will have discovered fire.

Jungian Insights

In her book, *Masks of the Soul*, Jung's former patient and later interpreter, Jolande Jacobi, put it this way:

> People are less and less willing to face the fact that God created the two sexes quite different, with different wave lengths, different means of expressing themselves, and different ways of loving. It is easy to make snap judgments of others based on oneself, and women's current drive for absolute equality with men shows that they think they can be like men if only they have the will for it. This, however, is simply not true. The basic difference cannot be eradicated, though it can be distorted to the detriment of human relationships. Every human being is, to some extent both a man and a woman . . . Every man carries his Eve within himself, and every woman her Adam. As a result of this duality we relate to each other not only through the sex we consciously belong to, but also transversely through our unconscious, contrasexual side.

Here I want to take the liberty of quoting from my book *The Gentle Art of Spiritual Guidance* to present my current thinking regarding how to relate this approach to homosexuality:

> These marks of the Spirit to which I am holding as the best criteria for judging the quality of an overt sexual relationship apply to homosexual relationships as well. This means that many individual homosexual unions, judged by these standards, are far superior to many an individual heterosexual union. I have known homosexual marriages that reflect the harvest of the Spirit in high degree. It is for homosexuals to comment on how this mythology applies to their orientation, if they see it as relevant. But I feel I must point out that in the Jungian context of the new mythology I am advocating, the degree of individuation ultimately attainable is likely to be more limited, generally speaking, when the interior masculine and feminine components are drawn into lively response only by another of the same sex.
>
> Moreover, the organic mandala made possible through the dynamic interaction between two persons of the same sex, while in given instances

no doubt of a better quality than a given heterosexual relationship, cannot, by reason of its obvious limitation, generally attain the same richness of pattern, or so it seems to me. With reference to the full human potential and depending upon the capacity of the individual, homosexuality may also be seen as a form of arrested development, whatever the complex causes. Depending on the depth and permanence of the orientation, in given instances the homosexual relationship may represent the only context within which any real development can take place. We do have a responsibility, I believe, assuming that all children and adults have a bisexual potential in varying degree, to encourage when possible the heterosexual development for the sake of realizing greater individuation and, potentially, a still richer union with another human being of the opposite sex.

This is not to disparage homosexuality. I hope I have made it clear that homosexuals should be judged by the same standards as heterosexuals. One of the good things that has come from the sexual revolution is that homosexuality has emerged from the closet. There is far less prejudice, far more acceptance. This is to be observed in nearly every form of art, athletics, business and education. It is a far healthier thing to have something so controversial aired and discussed. Western culture, operating for so long on the basis of biblical references to sexuality, has benefited by the new openness.

On the other hand, the sexual revolution has encouraged experimentation in heterosexual relationships that are, I believe, dangerous. Evolution itself, or the God of evolution, had chosen for the human species monogamy over polygamy after considerable experimentation with patterns of family relationships. But there is more to it than that. Scientific research has demonstrated the intricate interrelatedness of the body and the psyche. Everything that we are in the body is reflected one way or another in the psyche. Ultimately they are one integrated living organism. The whole psychosomatic structure seems to be on a journey involving the question of consciousness-raising. The axis over which evolution moves, complexity consciousness, involves the direction of inner as well as outer integration in the microcosm of the self within.

These observed truths point to monogamy as that principle of psychic health that supports growth and the interests and principles of evolution itself. There are two movements in evolution—what might be called "ongoingness" and "upreachingness." Procreation serves the first demand, ongoingness. Upreachingness, that mysterious movement toward the next mutation in human evolution, perhaps "Homo spiritus," will require monogamy for the efficient realization of its objective. When the child is born and begins the steep ascent toward individuation, monogamy is the better instrument within which to foster the kind of evolutionary progress toward higher consciousness.

Extramarital relationship, far from contributing to the individuation of the persons concerned, tends to complexify without integrating these persons. Individuation is not aided, but made even more difficult. The ongoing group of the family circle is a more congenial and intimate atmosphere or milieu in which to raise the child. If the values cherished by evolution or evolution's God, differentiation, interiorization, and communion, continue to hold here, as I believe they do, then clearly monogamy is preferable to polygamy. Differentiation issuing in subtle differences can teach its lessons with more attention given to subtleties. One can feel more protected than if polygamy were the pattern or institution under whose aegis the growth were to take place.

Interiority, the second value advocated by evolution, is better served by monogamy. If the human being is to have a richer, deeper life, he or she can realize this depth primarily by two processes: analysis and prayer, especially contemplative prayer.

Finally, those who aspire to wholeness, and in whom there is a deliberate attempt at deepening the interior life through contemplative prayer and analysis, are "rainmakers." In the company of others, they facilitate and encourage a deeper communion. Once again monogamy is a structure which fosters readiness to enter into deeper communion.

There is a certain training in the art of listening and responding appropriately in the small family unit which is conducive to spiritual growth. It is clear that the purposes of evolution are better served by monogamy than polygamy. This is not to say that the purposes of evolution are not well-served by a well-individuated homosexual. And, in the eyes of God there is no distinction. God bestows love on the heterosexual and the homosexual alike. Insofar as judgment goes, the marks of the spirit are still the basis of evaluation. God dwells at the core of the self in both.

I have called this chapter "The Eternal Feminine" because whatever myth the individual comes to, there must be a central place for the feminine, a place in the very consciousness of both men and women. Dante had a place for Beatrice, upon whom he projected the eternal feminine, from his youth to the end of his life. It was Beatrice who started him on his own inner journey and who, in *The Divine Comedy*, led him into paradise. She continued as his companion right up to the white rose, the divine mandala which symbolized the integration of his life. Dante realized integration of the feminine and masculine and achieved individuation in his mature journey into God. It was the eternal feminine, embodied in Beatrice, and Dante's faithful response that brought him to paradise.

Amor and Psyche: The Feminine and Consciousness

In *Amor and Psyche*, the Jungian analyst Erich Neumann interprets the story of the Greek lovers, Eros and Psyche. Their lovemaking effected an animal paradise of sensuality in the dark. Eros wanted it to go on in the same way forever. But Psyche was drawn to higher consciousness. She had made a promise to Eros that she would never attempt to see him in the light. But the pull of higher consciousness was irresistible for her. Eros left her in anger. Psyche thereupon embarked on her own inward journey to unite unconsciousness with consciousness. This decision on her part proved efficacious for Eros as well, because Psyche passed arduous tests demanding creative use and integration of her masculine component before she could see Eros again. Her final test was the recognition of relatedness and love as the source of her deepest identity and individuation as a woman. It is her individuation, her fusion of sex and spirit, that wins her divinization and admission to the pantheon of the gods. In the end she has realized a new value as divine, one that even Aphrodite had not attained. It was a heroic task to achieve a higher form of consciousness. Neumann puts it this way:

> The embrace of Eros and Psyche in the darkness represents the elementary but unconscious attraction of opposites, which impersonally bestows life, but not yet human life. But the coming of light makes Eros "visible." It manifests the phenomenon of psychic love, hence of all human love, as the human and higher form of the archetype of relatedness. It is only the completion of Psyche's development, effected in the course of her search for the invisible Eros, that brings with it the highest manifestation of the archetype of relatedness: a divine Eros joined with a divine Psyche.
>
> Psyche's individual love for Eros as love in the light is not only an essential element, it is *the* essential element in feminine individuation. Feminine individuation and the spiritual development of the feminine—

and herein lies the basic significance of this myth—are always effected through love. Through Eros, through her love of him, Psyche develops not only toward him, but toward herself. . . . But the unique feature of Psyche's development is that she achieves her mission not directly but indirectly, that she performs her labors with the help of the masculine, but not as a masculine being.

It is significant that we speak of the feminine soul in men and women alike; in both it is feminine. In another place Neumann says:

Psyche dissolves her *participation mystique* with her partner and flings herself and him into the destiny of separation that is consciousness. Love as an expression of feminine wholeness is not possible in the dark, as a merely unconscious process; an authentic encounter with another involves consciousness, hence also the aspect of suffering and separation.

Psyche's act leads, then, to all the pain of individuation, in which a personality experiences itself in relation to a partner as something other, that is, as not only connected with the partner . . . With Psyche, then, there appears a needed love principle, in which the encounter between the feminine and masculine is revealed as the basis of individuation.

So we see that without the use of Jungian terminology, the ancient Greek myth supports (as an independent source from the collective unconscious) the dynamic which both the Teilhardian and Jungian mythologies articulate for us in contemporary terms. Sexuality in the human animal is to rise above the unconscious to the higher forms of consciousness, reflecting the marks of the spirit. Psyche does not love Eros less but infinitely more.

In the Greek myth Psyche's capacity to love Eros paradoxically grows stronger and more beautiful even as she experiences more "otherness" and individuation. It is not wider experience in overt lovemaking with others that produces personal growth in Psyche and that enables raised consciousness. Rather, it is her lifelong fidelity that simultaneously enriches the union and makes possible the more profound individuation of both. Teilhard, as we have recognized earlier, perceived the remarkable paradox in this kind of relatedness and identified in it the operation of the law that union differentiates. So Teilhard's insight into the development of spirit and sex and Jung's insight into the development of a new fruit of the spirit, individuation, from the encounter of the masculine and feminine—in other words from sex—fit well together.

What does all this have to say about our current quest for the basis of a new sexual morality related to a more profound spirituality? First it provides, I believe, a new and viable mythology which can motivate us in this personal and social quest, through fresh revelation about laws that are written by God upon our inward parts. We have referred to Teilhard's discovery of the law of complexity-consciousness by which spirit emerges from matter through sexuality in the continuing evolutionary process. Ever higher forms of union and human relatedness are evidence of this law in operation. Another law operative in human relationships emerging from the energy inherent in sex is, as we have seen, the law that "union differentiates." Jung recognized this as a facet of the process of individuation advanced by an abiding man-woman relationship. Its interior counterpart is integration by the man of his anima and the woman of her animus.

This mythology grows out of a new understanding of the human psyche. Its source and destiny on this earth support a more excellent way, an enduring and sexually exclusive relationship between one man and one woman as most conducive to growth in the life of the spirit for all who are not expressly called to the celibate life. This is not to say that many such relationships, begun in good faith, are not properly dissolved when they become mutually destructive. Nor it is to deny that homosexual relationships may provide the only sexual union open to many persons. We should support these unions when they further the life of the spirit by the same criteria we apply to heterosexual unions. Both heterosexual and homosexual marriages, whether legalized by civil or religious ceremony or not, if they are to meet the human potential for development in the life of the spirit, will be increasingly characterized by love, joy, peace, patience, kindness, goodness, fidelity, gentleness and self-control.

It is not difficult to see how this applies to sexuality. That form of sexual expression and union is best which effectively differentiates, for true union differentiates. Again that form of union is good which fosters and encourages the interiority and subjectivity of both, thus furthering individuation and a marriage of the masculine and feminine components in each individual. Where differentiation and real interiority are present, more profound communion is possible, communion of which sexual intercourse is the sacrament, "the outward and visible sign of the inward and spiritual grace." Clearly these values are furthered most by an exclusive relationship, and one in which the mutual commitment is abiding and unconditional.

Though the myth of Eros and Psyche is ancient and Greek in origin, it has a timeless and universal wisdom to impart. I unashamedly chose it and borrow it for use in my personal myth of meaning because it speaks to my condition regarding the nature of the feminine, the eternal feminine.

CHAPTER FIVE

On Living Into the Forgiven Life

William Blake is one of my favorite poets. He was a great visual artist as well. His representations of God and man and woman are stunning. He was also a very able natural psychologist. There is something about his message which had to wait until now for recognition, but it is surprising how many insights we attribute to modern depth psychology were anticipated by this man. He was a visionary, a prophet. He saw Jesus as a man and all of us as the children of God. Moreover, he was a profound contemplative and has taken his place with the greatest of the mystics.

Poetic Mysticism

Blake would have known what Tennyson was talking about in this short poem in which Tennyson speaks of the cosmic ''all'':

> Flower in the crannied wall
> I pluck you out of the crannies
> I hold you here, root and all, in my hand
> Little flower—but if I could understand
> What you are, root and all and all in all
> I should know what God and man is.

Wordsworth knew the same inner world that drew William Blake. This mystic bonding with nature was conveyed in his poem written

July 13, 1798, "Lines Composed a Few Miles Above Tintern Abbey":

> For I have learned
> To look on nature, not as in the hour
> Of thoughtless youth; but hearing oftentimes
> The still, sad music of humanity,
> Nor harsh nor grating, though of ample power
> To chasten and subdue. And I have felt
> A presence that disturbs me with the joy
> Of elevated thoughts; a sense sublime
> Of something far more deeply interfused,
> Whose dwelling is the light of setting suns,
> And the round ocean and the living air,
> And the blue sky, and in the mind of man:
> A motion and a spirit that impels
> All thinking things, all objects of all thought,
> And rolls through all things. Therefore am I still
> A lover of the meadows and the woods,
> And mountains; and of all that we behold
> From this green earth; of all the mighty world
> Of eye, and ear, both what they half create,
> And what perceive; well pleased to recognize
> In nature and the language of the sense
> The anchor of my purest thoughts, the nurse
> The guide, the guardian of my heart, and soul
> Of all my moral being.

Jesus on Forgiveness

One afternoon, returning from conducting a retreat, I chanced to pick up a paper-bound copy of Blake's poetry. A poem entitled "The Everlasting Gospel" seized my attention. It is prefaced by a prose paragraph which raised the interesting question: Is there anything in the teaching of Jesus that was absolutely new, that had not been anticipated by any of the ancients, Plato, Cicero, or any other? There follows Blake's own answer to this query: Only one, the importance Jesus attached to the forgiveness of sins.

This was a new idea to me and I was impelled to do some research. I reread the gospels. I was amazed at how accurate Blake's statement actually was. So accurate that I thought to myself how Jesus was really "into" forgiveness in a big way.

Peter comes to Jesus with much enthusiasm. He is confident of his own magnanimity and says, "Lord, how many times shall I forgive my enemy—until seven times?" This was the new standard established by the rabbis, so Peter thought he was safe in adopting this figure of seven times. But Jesus answers in this way: "Peter, I say unto you, not until seven times but until seventy times seven." In other words, "You are never to stop forgiving, Peter."

> When you have ought against your brother, go and make it right with him first, and then go to the altar and make your gift. And he entered into a ship, and passed over and came into his own city. And behold, they brought to him a man sick of the palsy, lying on a bed: and Jesus seeing this faith said unto the sick of the palsy, "Son, be of good cheer." And behold, certain of the scribes said within themselves, this man blasphemeth. And Jesus knowing their thoughts said, "Wherefore think ye evil in your hearts? For whether it is easier to say, 'Thy sins be forgiven thee' or to say, 'arise and walk?' But that ye may know that the Son of Man hath power on earth to forgive sins," (then saith he to the sick of the palsy), "Arise, take up thy bed, and go into thine house." And he arose and departed to his house. And when the multitudes saw it, they marveled, and glorified God, which had given such power unto men. (Matthew 9:1–8)

There are people today who are paralyzed and who might be healed if one who spoke with authority could pronounce with the same authority that they have been forgiven.

> Then said Jesus unto them again, "Peace be unto you: as my father hath sent me, even so send I you." And when he had said this he breathed on them, and saith unto them, "Receive ye the Holy Ghost. Whosoever sins ye remit, they are remitted unto them; and whosoever sins ye retain they are retained." (John 20:21–23)

It comes as a surprise that Jesus authorized this priestly function on their part, whereas elsewhere he says it is God only who forgives sins. Apparently the gift of the Holy Spirit is the power to forgive.

> Take heed to yourselves: If thy brother trespass against thee, rebuke him; and if he repent, forgive him. And if he trespass against thee seven times in a day, and seven times in a day turn again to thee, saying, "I repent;" thou shalt forgive him. (Luke 17:3–4)

Here is basically the same message that was given to Peter. One is never to stop forgiving.

Wherefore I may say unto you, All manner of sin and blasphemy shall be forgiven unto man; but the blasphemy against the Holy Ghost shall not be forgiven unto man. And whosoever speaketh a word against the Son of Man, it shall be forgiven him, but whosoever speaketh against the Holy Ghost, it shall not be forgiven him, neither in this world, neither in the world to come.

And when thou prayest, thou shalt not be as the hypocrites are—for they love to pray standing in the synagogues and in the corners of the streets, that they may be seen of men. Verily, I say to you, they have their reward. But thou, when thou pray enter into thy closet, and when thou hast shut thy door, pray to the Father which is in secret; and the Father which seeth in secret will reward thee openly.

But when you pray use not vain repetitions as the heathens do. They think they shall be heard for their much speaking. Be not, therefore, like them, for your Father knows what things ye have need of before ye ask him.

After this manner therefore pray ye: Our Father which art in heaven, hallowed be thy name. Thy kingdom come, thy will be done in earth as it is in heaven. Give us this day our daily bread. And forgive us our debts as we forgive our debtors. And lead us not into temptation, but deliver us from evil. Thine is the kingdom and the power and the glory, forever. Amen.

For if ye forgive men their trespasses, your heavenly Father will also forgive you. But if ye forgive not men their trespasses, neither will your Father forgive your trespasses. (Matthew 6:5-15).

I have always found it a strange thing that God's forgiveness is contingent on our forgiveness of other men and women. It seems a strange threat—but there it is. Again with still more emphasis:

And when ye stand praying, forgive, if ye have ought against any: that your Father also which is in heaven may forgive you your trespasses. But if you do not forgive, neither will your Father which is in heaven forgive you your trespasses. (Mark 11:25-26)

It seems God's forgiveness awaits reciprocal movement on the part of men and women. The reason must be that forgiveness is a transaction which must involve the offended, the offender, and God all together.

Therefore is the kingdom of heaven likened unto a certain king which would take account of his servants. And when he had begun to reckon, one was brought unto him which owed him ten thousand talents. But forasmuch he had not to pay, his lord commanded him to be sold, and his wife, and children, and all that he had and payment to be made. The servant therefore fell down and worshipped him saying, "Lord have patience with me and I will pay thee all." Then the lord of that servant was moved with compassion, and loosed him, and forgave him the debt.

But the same servant went out and found one of his fellow servants, which owed him an hundred pence, and he laid hands on him, and took him by the throat, saying, "Pay me that thou owest." And his fellow servant fell down at his feet, and besought him saying, "Have patience with me, and I will pay thee all." And he would not; but went and cast him into prison, till he should pay the debt. So when his fellow servants saw what was done, they were very sorry and came and told their lord all that was done. Thus his lord, after that he had called him, said unto him, "O thou wicked servant, I forgave thee all that debt because that thou desiredst me. Shouldest not thou have had compassion on thy fellow servant even as I had pity on thee?" And his lord was wroth, and delivered him to the tormentors, till he should pay all that was due unto him. So likewise shall my heavenly Father do also unto you, if ye from your hearts forgive not every one his brother their trespasses. (Matthew 18:23-35)

This parable puts the landlord in a bad light indeed. He is as harsh as the king. In another place, however, the characteristic compassion returns:

Then said Jesus, "Father, forgive them for they know not what they do." (Luke 23:34)

Perhaps we can learn more from another parable regarding Jesus' teaching on forgiveness:

And one of the Pharisees desired him that he would eat with him. And he went into the Pharisee's house, and sat down to meat. And behold, a woman in the city, which was a sinner, when she knew that Jesus sat at meat in the Pharisee's house, brought an alabaster box of ointment. And stood at his feet behind him weeping, and began to wash his feet with tears, and did wipe them with the hairs of her head, and kissed his feet, and anointed them with the ointment. Now when the Pharisee which had bidden him saw it, he spake within himself, saying, "This man, if he were a prophet, would have known who and what manner of woman this was that toucheth him, for she is a sinner." And Jesus answering said unto him, "Simon, I have something to say unto thee." And he saith, "Master, say on."

"There was a certain creditor which had two debtors—the one owed five hundred pence, and the other fifty. And when they had nothing to pay, he frankly forgave them both. Tell me, therefore, which of them will love him most?" Simon answered and said, "I suppose that he to whom he forgave most.'' And he said unto him, ''Thou hast judged rightly.'' And he turned to the woman and said unto Simon, ''Seest thou this woman? I entered into thine house, thou gavest me no water for my feet: but she hath washed my feet with tears, and wiped them with the hairs of her head. Thou gavest me no kiss: but this woman since the time I came in hath not ceased to kiss my feet. My head with oil thou didst not annoint: but this woman hath annointed my feet with ointment. Wherefore I say unto thee, her sins, which are many, are forgiven for she loved much. But to whom little is forgiven, the same loveth little,'' and he said unto her, ''Thy sins are forgiven.'' And they that sat at meat with him began to say within themselves, ''Who is this that forgiveth sins also.'' And he said to the woman, ''Thy faith hath saved thee. Go in peace.'' (Luke 7:36-50)

I will record here two other passages because they further attest how concerned Jesus was with the phenomenon of forgiveness.

And as they were eating, Jesus took bread, and blessed it, and brake it, and gave it to the disciples, and said, ''Take, eat; this is my body.'' And he took the cup, and gave it to them, saying, ''Drink ye all of it; for this is my blood of the new testament which is shed for many for the remission of sins.'' (Matthew 26:26-28)

This again is a testimony as to the importance Jesus attached to the forgiveness of sins. Finally, Jesus was so devoted to this element in his teaching that he commissioned the disciples to carry it to all nations.

Then opened he their understanding, that they might understand the scriptures. And said unto them, thus it is written, and thus it behooved Christ to suffer, and to rise from the dead the third day. And that repentance and remission of sins should be preached in his name among all nations, beginning at Jerusalem. (Luke 24:45-47)

There is also what is called the Parable of the Prodigal Son, but might more truly be called the Parable of the Forgiving Father.

And he said, a certain man had two sons: And the younger of them said to his father, ''Father, give me the portion of goods that falleth to me.'' And he divideth unto them his living. And not many days after the younger son gathered all together, and took his journey into a far country and there wasted his substance with riotous living. And when he had spent all, there arose a mighty famine in that land; and he began to be in want. And he went and joined himself to a citizen of that country, and he sent him into the fields to feed swine. And he would fain have filled his belly with the husks that the swine did eat: and no man gave unto him.
  And when he came to himself, he said, ''How many hired servants

have bread enough and to spare, and I perish with hunger! I will arise and go to my father, and will say unto him, 'Father, I have sinned against heaven, and before thee, and am no more worthy to be called thy son: make me as one of thy hired servants.'' And he arose, and came to his father. But when he was yet a great way off, his father saw him and had compassion, and ran, and fell on his neck, and kissed him. And the son said unto him, ''Father I have sinned against heaven, and in thy sight, and am no more worthy to be called thy son.'' But the father said to his servants, ''Bring the best robe, and put it on him; and put a ring on his hand, and shoes on his feet; and bring hither the fatted calf, and kill it, and let us eat and be merry; for this my son was dead and is alive again; he was lost, and is found.'' And they began to be merry.

Now his elder son was in the field; and as he came and drew nigh the house, he heard music and dancing. And he called one of the servants and asked what these things meant. But he said unto him, ''Thy brother is come; and thy father hath killed the fatted calf because he hath received him safe and sound.'' And he was angry and would not go in; therefore came his father out, and entreated him. And he answering said to his father, ''Lo these many years do I serve thee; neither transgressed I at any time thy commandment; and yet thou never gavest me a kid, that I might make merry with my friends: But as soon as this thy son has come which hath devoured thy living with harlots, thou hast killed for him the fatted calf.'' And he said unto him, ''Son thou art ever with me, and all that I have is thine. It was meet that we should make merry, and be glad, for this thy brother was dead and is alive again; and was lost and is found.'' (Luke 15:11–32)

I have selected these examples from similar passages in the Bible to give some idea of the extent of the happenings, teachings, and parables which show how important Jesus thought forgiveness was in building the kingdom within.

How does it come about that Jesus was so fascinated by the process of forgiveness? If he were just anybody we would find it natural to inquire into the background of the man, to see if there are some direct connections between early experiences and patterns in early childhood training that would give us indications of what would produce the flowering or outcome of these promises. And when we look for these, they are there. But they are presented indirectly. One has first to accept the humanity of Jesus. He was not half human, half divine. He was all human. He was more thoroughly human than other men. Shall we borrow one of Teilhard's words? He was more highly *hominized* than other men and women. The Church long ago decided in one of its colloquies that Jesus was both human and divine.

But we are taking the view that Jesus was a man. There was that of God in him, but so is there that of God in every other man and woman.

On the assumption that he was fully human, we are obliged to believe that he had a shadow side. The Church has always said that he was tempted in all respects like other men, but without sin. But no man or woman alive is tempted and wholly without sin. Jesus himself showed his moral standard in the area of sexuality. He said that "He that looketh upon a woman with lust has already committed adultery in his heart." If he were to apply this standard of judgment to himself, and we are sure he would have, then just as surely he was a sinner in his own eyes.

I cannot believe that he submitted to baptism by John in Jordan just to be an example to the disciples or that he was playacting for public relations reasons. He must have come forward because he wanted to be baptized and forgiven his sins. Not to have looked on a woman to lust after her at least once is not human. Not to have a shadow side is not to be human. My conclusion is that Jesus came forward because he passionately sought forgiveness. His admonition about anger is another case in point: "Be angry and sin not" is another standard very difficult, if not impossible, to achieve. (Ephesians 4:26)

When Jesus came forward and was baptized by John in Jordan, he was rewarded with an unforgettable mystical experience. A voice in the dark says, "Behold—this is my beloved son in whom I am well pleased." (Matthew 17:5) This is tantamount to saying that Jesus was loved unconditionally, without restrictions or reservations, a way in which only God can love. From that moment on he was gifted with a boundless energy and capacity for loving. First he had the mystical experience of *being loved*, then he found the capacity to love in abundant measure, without exhaustion. Jesus could love the unlovable. Witness his love for John. This was an instance of loving the unlovable.

The baptism and the miracle of being able to love in superlative measure illustrates what asking and accepting forgiveness does for someone. It releases love. "She has been forgiven much, therefore, she is able to love much." Jesus was able to love much because he had been forgiven much by God. The Apostle John loved much because he had been forgiven much. Jesus and John together began to forge a chain of forgiveness, the end of which has not yet been reached.

Evolution and Forgiveness

From the point of view of evolution, forgiveness is a very significant phenomenon. Below the level of sentience on the tree of life, when things fall apart and there is a failure to unite the elements that might have come together, everything falls back into chaos or the void. When animals clash in a human setting, such as a dog and cat, they seem to make it up and go on as before. But with the human species, as a gift from higher consciousness, there is the possibility of working things out on a higher plane. In other words, a failure at union can be accepted, and an effort at reconciliation can give the two a second chance. One can conceive of this only on the plane of higher consciousness. We have spoken of the values of evolution: differentiation, interiority, communion. Union differentiates. Union is deeper when there is a profound communion. And a genuine communion is possible when some measure of differentiation and interiority is attained. It is something which has developed out of the ''within'' of evolution itself. This ''within'' makes for the possibility of ongoing union, abiding relationships and the communion of differentiated beings.

When two persons want reconciliation through forgiveness, the whole cosmos is involved, and the energy springing from forgiveness is released for other forms of service. Forgiveness releases love for service. Forgiveness makes possible a deeper communion than that which existed before. One can begin to see another reason why forgiveness is so important. Its importance is on the scale of evolution and it springs from the Creator of evolution. It invariably releases love, and love is the energy of creation. ''She loves much because she has been forgiven much.''

Sometimes forgiveness is very difficult to complete. It would seem that the hardest thing is to learn to forgive one's self. If I cannot forgive myself some transgression once and for all, perhaps I can accept forgiveness for twenty-four hours. On the morrow I can do so again. To live the forgiven life for twenty-four hours at a time, that I can learn to do!

Forgiveness is the gentle art of reconciling two or more people. It involves readiness to remain unforgiven. But one must always stand ready to forgive, whether a request for forgiveness is forthcoming or not, and one must request forgiveness when one has offended another, whether one is forgiven or not. And one must await the forgiveness of God until the sacrament of reconciliation has taken place on the human plane.

The world awaits the advent of the politics of forgiveness. What would have been the reaction of the people in the Soviet Union had Ronald Reagan made public apology in his TV address to them for having said some time earlier that Russia was an evil empire. Suppose he had asked to be forgiven and said that he had been guilty of a projection.

Elizabeth Barrett Browning once wrote a poem about a new kind of statesmanship in which the diplomat would ask not merely whether a proposed policy was good for his nation, but whether it might "be harmful for a nation hard by." We have not risen to that degree of consciousness, but that day is coming. It was recently approached when the Minister of Foreign Affairs publicly apologized for Russian entry into Afghanistan, calling it a mistake.

It is little wonder that forgiveness was the great theme in the teaching of Jesus. It is of cosmic proportion in the world that is aborning. The world reached a new level of raised consciousness and nobility of spirit when Jesus uttered from the cross the words, "Father, forgive them for they know not what they do." (Luke 23:34)

Les Misérables

Theatre audiences all over the world have been deeply moved by performances of *Les Misérables* over the last few years. The title, as far as content is concerned, might well have been: "He Loves Much Because He Has Been Forgiven Much" or "Living Into the Forgiven Life." In Victor Hugo's masterpiece we watch the hero visibly grow in stature and in favor with God and man. Most of you will recall the plot of the twelve-hundred-page novel. I think the characterization of the hero, Jean Valjean, deserves to be ranked with the greatest in fiction such as Hamlet, Faust, and Don Quixote. The power of forgiveness to release love is the central theme running throughout the book.

You will remember how the story begins. Jean Valjean had been sentenced to serve nineteen years on a chain gang for stealing a loaf of bread for a nephew. He must wear a yellow tag for identification. He is trailed by the gendarme, Javert, for violation of probationary rules. Everyone scorns or ignores him save for one man: the Bishop of Digne, who bestows unconditional love on this criminal. The not yet converted Jean Valjean "rewards" the bishop by stealing some of his silver. He is apprehended and returned to be confronted by the offended. Javert would have him jailed again.

But the Bishop does the unbelievable. He quietly says to the gathered company, "I gave it to him." And, as if this were not enough to shock them all, he bestows on Jean Valjean a pair of silver candlesticks. That does it! This gesture blows the mind of Jean Valjean. From henceforth he lives into the forgiven life, going "from strength to strength in the life of perfect service." He makes a deathbed promise to Fantine that he will adopt her little daughter Cosette, a vow he keeps until she is married to Marius years later.

Javert is a complete opposite to Valjean. He identifies with his persona which he sees as a God-given mission to guard society from criminals like Jean Valjean. When Valjean spares his life and is prepared to forgive him, Javert has not a clue as to the meaning and power of forgiveness. The self-image no longer holds. "It's either Valjean or Javert." The world cannot hold both. He decides there is no longer a place for him and flings himself into the Seine.

Meanwhile, Valjean, who is, under another name, the owner of a factory and the mayor of a town, flees to Paris. There he rescues young Marius who is dying from a wound inflicted in an abortive student revolution. Valjean throws Marius over his shoulder and carries him through the sewers of Paris to safety.

One of the hardest things his love must transcend is jealousy of Marius, who has fallen in love with Cosette. He surmounts even this hurdle, transforming jealousy into acceptance with love, as he entrusts Cosette to Marius. At last, with death approaching, he reveals his identity and confesses to Marius that it was he who saved his life. After the marriage of Cosette to Marius, Jean Valjean is dying. Cosette is comforting him. His last words are appropriately, "Forgive me all my trespasses and take me to your glory." Notice that the tone is one of total confidence that he will be forgiven all his trespasses and of assurance that he can claim the right to be taken to God's glory. He quietly passes over to the other side where he finds himself to be in the company of Fantine and the students who died in the revolution. A touching line, perhaps the most moving in the entire drama, is chanted by the chorus: "To love another person is to see the face of God."

One who loves much has been forgiven much, and one who has been forgiven much loves much. The power of forgiveness to release love is a great new phenomenon on the scale of evolution. "If you forgive your brother and sister, your heavenly Father will forgive you."

CHAPTER SIX

Intimations of Immortality

The human being has a curious capacity to put out of mind what does not seem relevant to the present moment. Unless one has been afflicted with some terminal illness which confronts one with the probability of imminent death, the psyche has a way of postponing reflection on its own ultimate demise. It may be that the death of a loved one demands that one pay attention, at least for a season, to this great mystery which has through bereavement altered the course of one's own interior life forever.

In the process of grieving one is compelled to reflect on the meaning of death in order to come to some kind of terms with the intense loneliness and emptiness which inevitably ensues. But short of such provocation one usually finds it convenient to wait until the advancing years of old age require that one take an inward stand, accept some form of a traditional myth or undertake to shape a new one that bears some plausibility in the light of present knowledge and fresh revelation. It would seem that until one is faced with a sense of the "eleventh hour," the solitary individual does not feel an urgent need to come to personal convictions regarding death.

Our Contemporary Source of Doubt

There was a time when there was general acceptance on the part of those who saw themselves as standing in the Christian tradition of the inherited myth involving consignment hereafter to one of three places: hell, purgatory, or paradise. There was some difference of opinion as to whether this took place immediately after death or at the end of the world; but that a final judgment was involved and that this judgment was irrevocable was taken for granted. The great myth was given consummate expression in Dante's *Divine Comedy* and Doré provided the accompanying etchings that seared their way into the memories of the impressionable. I can remember as a child the mortal terror that afflicted me when I turned the pages of the large volume entitled *Dante's Inferno*. It was left, I have always suspected, on the library table by my father and mother, with deliberate intent for the edification of us children.

Confident, on many counts, that I would ultimately by consigned to hell, I remember vividly with what present torment I tried to decide, if I were given a choice (which I was confident I wouldn't be), which punishment I would prefer of the various forms offered. I could never make up my mind which would be worse: to spend all eternity in those private pits from which flames issued or to be confined to a cubicle of ice from which only my feet protruded. Either image was enough to make my flesh creep and to produce horrendous nightmares. If release from the fear of such torment were the only benefit bestowed by the Age of Enlightenment, we should have just cause for celebrating such liberation.

I doubt whether there would be more than a few among those reading this book who are disturbed by concern for where they might be assigned after death in terms of heaven, hell or purgatory. Before we boast of our comparative liberation, let us acknowledge our own peculiar brand of fear associated with death. We do not waste much energy, if any, over an anxiety as to whether we shall have to stand judgment for our sins on death and anticipate appropriate punishment or reward. For many of us, our anxiety has a different origin, but it is doubtful whether it is any less intense than that suffered by our grandparents. Our problem with regard to the death of our loved ones and our own inescapably approaching death is a besetting doubt as to whether there is any personal survival whatever.

We are constrained to see death in a new context: the demonstrable psychosomatic unity of life. We are so fully persuaded that the body and the psyche are one that we have come to expect that anything that affects the body will alter the condition of the psyche and vice versa. It is hard for us to imagine that when the lifeless body lies in decay, the psyche or soul can still be alive. The personality of our beloved is such an integral entity, combining a measure of health or illness with subtle expressions of the familiar countenance, changing moods and psychological states, that we are hard put to imagine what form the person could take once the body is no longer there to clothe it. It is important to us to keep our universe a universe. Strong as our instinctive need is for reassurance that the beloved survives death in some form, still greater is our need to keep our world one and to abide by empirical reasoning. We are prepared to forego this comfort rather than be guilty of wishful thinking that can muster no scientific support. So profoundly have we been influenced by the age of science in which we live! If we are no longer fearful of a final judgment in which we may not fare well, some of us are utterly dismayed that a still worse fate may await us at death— oblivion as far as any recognizable remnant of our person is concerned.

We are not only saddened by this possibility; it sometimes provokes a deep anger within us. The thought that what I have given my best energy to for so long may at death suffer a final dissolution or entropy evokes a sense of betrayal. What kind of God would induce me to be a co-creator of my own individuated self over so long a period and at such a price in suffering only to end peremptorily the whole enterprise in nothingness? Contemporary man and woman are required to ponder such unsettling considerations. There is no sidestepping them. Death has not chosen thus far to reveal its secrets. I believe, as I trust many of you do, that there is no definitive proof of personal survival. Then how shall we live a radiant and confident life in the presence of such profound doubt concerning the possibility of personal immortality? Without positive assurance of life after death, can this life any longer hold a numinous candle for us? This is the heart of our query. Are there any intimations in which we can put our ultimate confidence? And if not, is there any principle or experience in which we can put our trust?

Purported Proofs of Immortality

There are a variety of experiences of a psychic nature which are commonly considered as strong evidence, if not actual proof, of life after death. While I respect the sincerity of most of those who advance these so-called ''proofs,'' and intend to retain an open mind regarding the interpretation of such experiences, I must confess that none until now is fully persuasive to me. I find that there is always one more question to be asked, the answer to which is not yet forthcoming.

Consider first the fairly common experience of déjà vu, which convinces many of what has historically been called reincarnation. I suppose that most of us have had comparable experiences suggesting we have lived in a different place in an earlier life, so familiar does a geographic setting seem when first visited in this life. And who has not had a strange sense that one has known another person before, perhaps in an earlier life, so hauntingly familiar is the countenance and manner, though one knows for certain there has been no prior meeting in this life?

There is something very appealing about the doctrine of reincarnation, especially as an opportunity to compensate for inequalities in this life. The idea of karma, a working out over the span of a number of lifetimes, wrongs committed in a given life, is one of the corollaries of this position regarding immortality. Part of the appeal is that it seems much more compassionate and merciful a way to right wrongs, make up for inequalities of opportunity, and a chance to "do penance" in a more creative way than the Christian dogma of heaven and hell allows. The latter may seem just but lacks comparable mercy.

Some versions add the attractive notion that one can choose one's parents in the next life, though this "bonus" has rarely been claimed and been appreciated in the event. Even if one were persuaded on spiritual grounds, there are statistical grounds that give rise to doubts as to the practicality of such a scheme in an evolving universe and with an expanding species. But the source of my own doubts springs from my own firm conviction as to the reality of a dynamic affecting the human psyche to which C. G. Jung has given the name "collective unconscious." It seems to me that such experiences as we have just alluded to might be accounted for as springing up into consciousness from that vast sea connecting the living and their recollection of the dead in the unconscious, that sea, as one of the poets has told us, "from whose bourne no traveller returns." This may be the very reason that Jung, while admittedly tempted to believe in reincarnation, did not in the end claim it as an article of faith.

There are also the spiritualists who claim through mediums to be able to put one in direct touch with the souls of departed loved ones. Some of these mediums have been exposed as charlatans. Some have seemed credible. Two considerations here give me pause: the excessive need of the client to communicate with the departed (causing possible projection), and the too often banal character of the life represented by the medium as existing "on the other side." In the accounts I have read the thought has occurred to me that if that is what it is like beyond the grave, I am not sure I want to go! It reaffirms my preference for this life and I find myself confirming the poignant words of Robert Frost, "I don't know where it's likely to go better."

A more up-to-date version of what has usually gone by the name of spiritualism is the phenomenon of so-called "channeling," sometimes associated with the charismatic movement. The counseling offered is often remarkably relevant and there is persuasive evidence at times of clairvoyance on the part of the channel. Yet here again, there would appear to be the possibility of psychic activity emerging out of the personal unconscious as well as the collective unconscious. Again, when presented in such an appealing way by someone like Shirley MacLaine, I am prompted to acknowledge, "Almost thou dost persuade me!" Something of great value to the psyche of the person involved is apparently happening. There is the admitted presence of love, tenderness, compassion, considerateness; all these. And yet I am aware that there are elements present which could be understood as psychic phenomena arising from the personal and collective unconscious. These phenomena do not necessarily confirm the reality of what is transpiring as literally true. Moreover, sometimes grave temptations to inflation threaten the integrity of the medium.

In the past few years there have been popular books published which amass evidence supporting the case for immortality by recounting experiences of persons pronounced dead who have returned to life. Elisabeth Kübler-Ross and Raymond L. Moody are among these reputable writers. The experiences speak of brief sojourns in a transitional state between life and death when the person appears to have left the body temporarily but has not yet arrived at the state of life after death. I knew a doctor in charge of medical services for students for a number of years at Harvard University, Alfred Worcester, who claimed to have witnessed after-death experiences of his patients and to have undergone a similar experience himself during a near-fatal sickness.

In his autobiography, *Memories, Dreams, Reflections*, Jung shares an "out-of-the-body" experience during a serious illness which would fall in this category, though he does not expressly claim for it a life-after-death revelatory quality. These accumulated testimonies from so many credible subjects are impressive. And yet I must respond,

''How can one be sure that the experiences which are purported to be of an after-death nature are not, in fact, emanating from the unconscious where they have been initially deposited as repressed bits of fantasy and active imagination?''

As a pastor, over a period of twenty years, I often had occasion to be at the bedside of a dying person in the company of members of the family. It was my practice to try to be present at the moment of death in order to be of some comfort, it may be, to those about to be bereaved. Out of personal experience I could confirm another claim of Dr. Worcester that it not infrequently happened that as death approached the patient became more conscious of the presence of departed loved ones than of living friends or relatives keeping vigil in the room. One could easily assume that such experiences prove that the dying person was already nearer to other departed souls than to the living. Perhaps I am of an overly skeptical nature and have been too well-trained in the critical discipline of empirical science, but I have never been able to exclude the possibility that such phenomena could be accounted for on the ground of access to the patient's unconscious through a kind of dreaming that amounted to hallucination. But I am willing to concede that there may be a borderline of convergence or overlapping between an after death existence and the unconscious in some of its capabilities and manifestations.

I want to interject here the fact that I do believe in the phenomena of clairvoyance and telepathy between living persons. Instances are so well-documented as to defy refutation. And most of us, I am persuaded, have had minor experiences of extrasensory perception. If one posits life after death, some continuation of consciousness, then it would seem quite likely that telepathic communication might well be possible between the living and the dead, especially among persons who had been very close to each other in this life. But I would have to insist that there is no way of being certain, in given instances, whether or not the living person is communicating with some personalized figures derived from repressed or suppressed memories in the unconscious. This is more plausible than that communication takes place with the consciousness, retained after death, of the other person. I must conclude, in the present state of my own reflection, once again, that while some of the evidence submitted by contemporary writers having to do with communication between the living and the dead seems plausible, one cannot be certain it is authentic, as presented. I confess to being envious of those who are able to place confidence unreservedly in such evidence, but I am not among them.

Intimations Arising from Naturalistic Evidence

Not long ago my attention was drawn to a book entitled *A Matter of Personal Survival: Life After Death* by Michael Marsh, a much respected member of the Religious Society of Friends. The book represents the publication of a doctoral dissertation in the Department of Philosophy at Catholic University in Washington D.C. Marsh calls himself an empiricist and combines this discipline with that of philosophy. It is not surprising, then, that he approaches the question of personal survival with a focus of attention on naturalistic evidence and submits his final judgment of the probability of life after death on a careful analysis of this evidence.

His argument runs something like this. Brain surgeons have located many of the functions of the psyche in various parts of the physical brain. The science of the brain has gone far beyond the concept of the bicameral division that has become familiar to us as left-brain, right-brain functions. But there are two aspects of the psyche that have not yet been located in the physical brain: what Marsh calls pure memories and what we commonly refer to as the "inmost self." The question is where these two aspects of the psyche are stored, and the suggestion is that they are stored in that part of the mind whose dimensions are not co-terminous with the brain. The assumption is that the mind is larger than the brain and at the same time contains or makes use of the brain. It is also suggested that it is this part of the mind which contains the element of consciousness that survives death. With C. G. Jung, Marsh would hold that personal survival of death requires survival of some form of individual consciousness.

I do not pretend to follow the subtleties of Marsh's scientific argument here. I do not know enough about the science of the brain, but I am fascinated by this whole idea about the existence of a part of the mind that transcends the charted functions of the brain. Marsh recognizes that the death of the body, inclusive of the brain, would severely limit the aspects of the personality that can survive death. His is a fascinating approach because of the commitment to stay with empirical evidence. Marsh speaks of plausibility, not certainty, and brings his quest to a close with these words:

I believe an overall judgment of moderately plausible is now warranted for personal survival after death, based on the naturalistic grounds we have explored. To claim high plausibility, overall, seems dubious because so many of the points at issue have only moderate plausibility in their favor. It seems clear, however, that the sum of all the evidence opening the way to survival is very substantial, and that it outweighs the opposing evidence. Thus the assertion of moderate plausibility for survival appears warranted.

Marsh calls his approach the "full-life view." His phrase "the inmost self" might be equated with the word "soul," which has during much of Christian history connoted that part of the psyche which is eternal. He describes the difference such a belief makes in one's life:

No doubt the effect of such a belief will differ if one comes into it from faith rather than by climbing up out of a reductionist world view, as happened with me. In the latter case, as one absorbs the full-life hypothesis into belief, along with a foundational belief in the inward light, the whole tone of one's life begins to shift. The sense of boredom, drudgery, meaningless "anomie" falls away. It is as if one has been living in a city with polluted air and then moved to a place with pure air.

In addition to this change, the survival belief may serve as an emotional safety net. However well we are functioning, moments do arrive when things go wrong. Crises of feeling flare up. We may find ourself treated unjustly. We may be forced to seek a new job, or to consider divorce, or face life crippled and in pain. We may be assaulted, or we may discover ourself acting shamefully. We may begin to feel crushed, helpless, bereft. In such bitter times, the knowledge that this painful experience is not all of us—that the everlasting inmost self persists, holding the whole core of us since childhood—can help to rescue our consciousness from despair. This, too, shall pass: and our true self remains. We have no need to fear the world for the world cannot destroy us. Moreover, those loved ones now gone who once consoled us still await us in the end.

Perhaps the greatest insight of the full-life belief is that each human being has a meaning. We humans exist not merely as momentary collections of atoms, tiny fluxes of mass/energy in a heedless universe, but also as enduring noetic beings in another less alien realm. Moreover, the meaning of life is unique. It is not duplicated by any other life, for the situation in which each of us functions is not like any other's.

And to whom do we answer for our life? So far as naturalistic inquiry can tell us, we answer primarily to our own inmost self and its subjective "I." But that is the self which endures, which outlasts our organism, which seeks meanings and which eventually will uncover all these meanings—flawed, failed, and sweetly realized—that we have presented to it by living our life. It will uncover those meanings and will judge them, and then go on. But beyond our self there may be a greater, and a loving, and eternal, judge.

Certainly I must agree with Marsh that if we can with integrity accept, still more embrace with enthusiam, a myth of personal survival, it will make a difference in the quality and the level of responsibility with which we live this life. But, alas, abstract truth does not of itself persuade us of the reality of immortality. I am glad an empirical philosopher finds reassurance of life after death in this "full-life" theory based on naturalistic inquiry. And I happily commend this book to others. But some of us will have to look elsewhere as well for intimations that are persuasive and for a modus vivendi, vis-à-vis death, that will constitute a creative way of accepting the possibility that there is no recognizable personal survival.

Intimations from the Perspective of Evolution

For some time now, as I explained in Chapter 5, I have been corresponding with an Indian priest in the Anglican Communion who lives in Pondicherry, India. Many years ago, when Sri Aurobindo was still alive, the friend, whom I have never met, was drawn to the Aurobindo Ashram by the teaching of this Hindu philosopher. Educated in England and inspired by the revelation of the fact of continuing creation through evolution, Aurobindo did for Hindu thought what Teilhard de Chardin did for Christian thought. He assimilated into it the evolutionary perspective, thereby achieving an updating within the Hindu context. My friend, M. P. John, was profoundly influenced by Aurobindo's ideas, especially as they were presented in the epic poem *The Life Divine*.

Not long ago, as I indicated earlier, M. P. John sent me a copy of his recent book, *In Defense of Death*. With his Indian background it is not surprising that John accepts the reincarnation myth and reminds us that there were those in the Christian Church who believed in reincarnation until the doctrine was pronounced "anathema" at the Second Council of Constantinople in A.D. 553. What is especially refreshing about his treatise is that he approaches his inquiry into life after death from the perspective of evolution. He would agree with Teilhard that evolution is "a light illuminating all facts . . . a curve which henceforth all lines must follow." From now on any viable myth concerning life after death will have to be articulated with reference to what we know about evolution. For John, death is the entrance to a new state of consciousness. We are not to anticipate a physical resurrection but an opportunity to continue to evolve. In the light of evolution the lines of our thought about death must begin to follow that curve. To quote again from M. P. John's book, *In Defense of Death*:

> Evolution of Consciousness is what should engage our attention.
> In the beginning was the Principle of Evolution and the Principle of Evolution was God. All things were made by Evolution and without Evolution was not anything made that was made. In Evolution was Life, and the Life was the light of men.
> Today it becomes necessary to think of God in terms of Evolution. The life that is in each of us is the manifestation of Evolution, the God within.
> I am not referring to Darwin's theory of physical evolution. I am referring to the Evolution of Consciousness. The stage of Consciousness determines the nature of the body required for the evolution of Consciousness. The Principle of Evolution implies infinite possibilities, and here or there one form of life breaks through to the next stage.

Darwin perceived the continuity of all life once the first cell had been created. Teilhard went deeper and perceived the continuity between pre-life and life. Darwin studied the physical ascent of life. Teilhard recognized the "within" of things, and conjectured that consciousness must already be present in its most primitive form at the heart of matter. If this hypothesis be accepted, then we are all at least as old as the planet itself, and our origin reaches back into the very stardust of our galaxy. In other words there is that in us which has been immortal until now.

The seed of our present being lay asleep in matter from the beginning. This insight supports the conviction of all the mystics that God is immanent in each one of us in a wholly original, never to be repeated, way. Whatever happens to us at death, it seems unlikely that a continuity maintained for so long should suddenly be ended by death. It was Teilhard's recurring mystical experience to see that God was "the diaphany of the divine at the heart of the universe on fire." This God at the heart of our being, intimately and paradoxically fused with our self, the very Self of ourself, must be immortal.

We may at least claim this measure of immortality: the immortal God within us will not die when we die.

But the unique individual that I am, which makes me different even from my twin brother and by which my friends recognize me, my personality, will that survive death? That is a question which it seems to me cannot be answered unequivocally. Will one I have "loved long since and lost awhile" be known to me again when I too cross the bar? This is the instinctive longing of my heart. But I confess I look in vain for incontrovertible evidence here.

One thing is clear to me on the principle that we live in a universe that is dependable, consistent, even "infallible," as Teilhard noted. If my being retains integrity and continuity at death I shall continue to evolve. It is utterly inconceivable that at the death of my body my consciousness should survive in some static form, frozen for all time in some fixed condition that continues what I then was or will be. Assuming personal survival, had we the clairvoyance to see or the omniscience to communicate with the historic Abraham Lincoln or Thomas Jefferson, would they be the same now as they were at their death? Clearly, in the context of an evolving universe, this is unthinkable.

Still pondering, in this perspective of space-time that the process of evolution affords, what right have I to claim for the human species a privilege that I do not insist upon for the rest of the animal world to which I am so intimately related? I have had an Afghan hound of singular beauty and grace, who, I fancied, was my superior in the art of contemplation, and an Irish Setter whose gentleness and long-suffering were attested by the sadness and patience in her eyes. Would a God who generously bestowed immortality on me by prolonging my being beyond the grave deny this benefit to my fellow creature whose spirit, it seems to me, is more deserving than my own? If I am going to be able "to walk all over God's heaven," should not my Afghan and Irish Setter be allowed to wander, unconfined, over green pastures on endless rolling hills? Pascal knew that the heart has its reasons which the mind cannot comprehend. And the heart demands justice of the mind. These considerations also give me pause when it comes to an uncritical acceptance of the inherited Christian myth.

The myth that does hold me captive still is Teilhard's myth of cosmogenesis, a cosmos still being born. With M. P. John, my credo begins, "I believe in the Principle of Evolution, the Maker of heaven and earth and the evolving man." I believe in the law Teilhard discerned as operative in continuing creation through evolution: the law of complexity consciousness. I believe that this process has a direction, that it unfailingly moves toward the creation of higher consciousness. It may be that personal survival of the phenomenon of death is a gift imparted to those who have attained higher consciousness in this life. But the demand of justice I impose on God would preclude an immortality reserved for those whose endowment and opportunity to attain higher consciousness were greater than others. It must be a condition granted to all or none. We can safely assume that evolution is striving toward higher consciousness, but is the death of the body an entrance to such a realm for the soul? I do not think it is given us to know, not as yet anyway.

Wordsworth's Intimations of Immortality from Early Childhood

Let us then pursue another path of active imagination, one which was charted for us by William Wordsworth in a poem which has until now enjoyed its own form of immortality: "Ode: Intimations of Immortality from Recollections of Early Childhood." It was composed between 1805 and 1807 at the peak of his powers and before the decline of his genius. We note that this was also before Darwin. Wordsworth could not have known anything about evolution. Yet I think that he intuited something comparable: a progression from the distant past that is present in the spirit of the child who somehow retains a marvelous recall. I do not think that Wordsworth is talking about reincarnation, but something closer to evolution, when he sees the child as "trailing clouds of glory" and "coming from God who is our home." The poet is witnessing the internal experience of having been immortal until now. He is not at all interested, in this poem at least, in intimations of immortality garnered from the kind of psychic experiences purporting to give evidence of life after death which we were examining earlier, even though there must have been comparable testimony among some of his contemporaries. He is interested in the child's consciousness of beauty and of glory that the child brings from an earlier state.

Initially the poet is troubled by a nagging nostalgia:

> There was a time when meadow, grove, and stream,
> The earth, and every common sight,
> To me did seem,

Apparelled in celestial light,
The glory and the freshness of a dream.
It is not as it hath been of yore—
Turn whereso'er I may,
By night or day,
The things which I have seen I now can see no more.

Wordsworth embarks on a dialogue with himself in which he expresses his ambivalence. He concedes, in response to the blessed creatures he once knew so intimately, that there still is a sense in which

My heart is at your festival,
My head hath its coronal,
The fullness of your bliss, I feel—I feel it all.

And to be unappreciative or in mourning at such a time seems inappropriate:

Oh, evil day! if I were sullen
While Earth herself is adorning,
This sweet May morning,
And the children are culling
On every side,
In a thousand valleys far and wide,
Fresh flowers; while the sun shines warm,
And the babe leaps up on his Mother's arm—
I hear, I hear, with joy I hear!

And yet, and yet, the nostalgia persists:

—But there's a Tree, of many, one,
A single Field which I have looked upon,
Both of them speak of something that is gone:
The Pansy at my feet
Doth the same tale repeat:
Whither is fled the visionary gleam?
Where is it now, the glory and the dream?

He then reflects and posits a plausible answer to this query:

Our birth is but a sleep and a forgetting:
The Soul that rises with us, our life's Star,
Hath had elsewhere its setting,
And cometh from afar:
Not in entire forgetfulness,
And not in utter nakedness,

> But trailing clouds of glory do we come
> From God, who is our home:
> Heaven lies about us in our infancy!
> Shades of the prison-house begin to close
> Upon the growing Boy
> But He beholds the light, and whence it flows,
> He sees it in his joy;
> The Youth, who daily farther from the east
> Must travel, still is Nature's Priest,
> And by the vision splendid
> Is on his way attended;
> At length the Man perceives it die away,
> And fade into the light of common day.

The tension between the opposites begins to mount. Something would appear to be lost. And yet not only the memory but the present experience of glory keeps coming back. The earth . . .

> The homely Nurse doth all she can
> To make her foster child, her Inmate Man,
> Forget the glories he hath known,
> And that imperial palace whence he came.

It is as if "his whole vocation were endless imitation," so consumed by the collective does he become, so difficult is the path of individuation. There follows a tribute to the child that is a veritable paean of praise. It is the turning point of the poem because one is dimly aware that, after the manner of poets, who are entitled to speak on more than one level at once, Wordsworth is also speaking of the inner child in everyone, the "puer aeternus," perhaps the Christ child within:

> Thou, whose exterior semblence doth belie
> Thy Soul's immensity;
> Thou best Philosopher, who yet doest keep
> Thy heritage, thou Eye among the blind,
> That, deaf and silent, read'st the eternal deep,
> Haunted forever by the eternal mind—
> Mighty Prophet! Seer Blest!
> On whom those truths do rest,
> Which we are toiling all our lives to find,
> In darkness lost, the darkness of the grave;

Thou, over whom thy Immortality
Broods like the Day, a Master o'er a Slave.

Wordsworth feels the poignancy and infinite pathos of what awaits this child:

Full soon thy Soul shall have her earthly freight,
And custom lie upon thee with a weight,
Heavy as frost, and deep almost as life!

Even so, the inner child is still there and once again informs the soul of its immortal past:

O joy! that in our embers
Is something that doth live,
That nature yet remembers
What was so fugitive!

Wordsworth seems to anticipate Jung's idea of "midlife crisis" when he raises a song of thanks and praise:

. . . for those obstinate questionings
Of sense and outward things,
Fallings from us, vanishings;
Blank misgivings of a Creature
Moving about in worlds not realized,
High instincts before which our mortal Nature
Did tremble like a guilty Thing surprised.

The poet even foresees a resolution to this midlife crisis:

Hence in a season of calm weather
Though inland far we be,
Our Souls have sight of that immortal sea
Which brought us hither,
Can in a moment travel thither,
And see the Children sport upon the shore,
And hear the mighty waters rolling evermore.

A gift has been granted to the seeker which more than compensates for any loss:

What though the radiance which was once so bright
Be now forever taken from my sight,
Though nothing can bring back the hour
Of splendor in the grass, of glory in the flower;
We will grieve not, rather find

> Strength in what remains behind;
> In the primal sympathy
> Which having been must ever be;
> In the soothing thoughts that spring
> Out of human suffering;
> In the faith that looks through death,
> In years that bring the philosophic mind.

One of the extraordinary things about this particular insight of Wordsworth's is that the poet was only thirty-three when he wrote this remarkable poem. He exercised the poet-prophet's license to anticipate a truth in advance of the experience. The gift which is granted sometimes to the aging when a sufficient level of consciousness has been attained, the philosophic mind, I am persuaded, can be equated with the contemplative mind to which the living religions aspire.

The poet admits to the elements that he has relinquished only one delight:

> To live beneath your more habitual sway.

For this loss there is more than ample compensation:

> I love the Brooks which down their channels fret,
> Even more than when I tripped lightly as they;
> The innocent brightness of a newborn Day
> Is lovely yet;
> The clouds that gather around the setting sun
> Do take a sober coloring from an eye
> That hath kept watch o'er man's mortality.

The poet holds no brief in this poem specifically for personal survival of death as such. Indeed, in his closing words he prefers to acknowledge having ''kept watch over man's mortality.'' He points to the unexpected gift of aging: the capacity to take delight in others' achievements, letting go of the spirit of competition and the ego's restless aspiration to excel, and being content to entrust oneself to a sense of ''kinship with all things'':

> Another race hath been, and other palms are won.
> Thanks to the human heart by which we live,
> Thanks to its tenderness, its joys, and fears,
> To me the meanest flower that blows can give
> Thoughts that do often lie too deep for tears.

What Wordsworth is really talking about, it seems to me, is the recurring mystical experience of being loved by the Creator, of being one with all creation, and of the interpenetration of all things. In other words, the experience, from time to time, of life eternal. The real intimation of immortality is not some purported proof of life after death but the experience here and now of timelessness, the glory and the dream of life eternal.

The Ego's Last Stand

The ego is that in us which, as the author of the *Theologica Germanica* recognized, is constantly clamoring about "the I, the me, the mine, and the like." And well might this ego be anxious about death since whatever else death may demand of us it is certain to say with regard to everything we think we possess, "You can't take it with you!" From the point of view of the ego, death is the great and final diminishment. No wonder this ego of ours puts up such a violent protest. It naturally refuses to "go gentle into that good night."

The self is a different matter. The self is the proximation toward wholeness, the totality of what we are in this life, our measure of achievement of individuation or differentiation from all other men and women who now are or who have ever been. And yet this self is paradoxically one with the Self, God within. This mysterious and indescribable union is what mystical experience discloses at its peak. "I and the Father are one," said Jesus. "My me is God," said St. Catherine of Siena and Meister Eckhart. As surely as the body decomposes, "earth to earth, ashes to ashes, dust to dust," the self must return in some sense to the Self, God. How this can be and how it is realized is something we cannot even begin to imagine. But there is that in us which insists it must be so.

There is a school of mysticism, East and West, which holds that our individuality, in the sense of a separate soul, is an illusion. Not only is no one an island in terms of complete isolation in this life—that all are part of the main—but also our deaths do not isolate us from others. The self in terms of an individuated consciousness may indeed dissolve into the universal consciousness, the Alpha and Omega, who is God. This possibility is precisely what the ego cannot accept; but from the point of view of the self, which has already experienced its unity both with other selves and with the Self, it would simply be a matter of going home.

Perhaps the words which conclude the autobiography of C. G. Jung can be understood as a premonition, an intuition of the approaching transformation already anticipated in the psyche:

> When Lao-tzu says: "All are clear, I alone am clouded," he is expressing what I feel now in advanced old age. Lao-tzu is the example of a man with superior insight who has seen and experienced worth and worthlessness, and who at the end of his life desires to return into his own being, into the eternal unknowable meaning. The archetype of the old man who has seen enough is eternally true. At every level of intelligence this type appears, and its lineaments are always the same, whether it be an old peasant or a great philosopher like Lao-tzu. This is old age, and a limitation. Yet there is so much that fills me: plants, animals, clouds, day and night, and the eternal in man. The more uncertain I have felt about myself, the more there has grown up in me a feeling of kinship with all things. In fact it seems to me as if that alienation which so long separated me from the world has become transferred into my own inner world, and has revealed to me an unexpected unfamiliarity with myself.

What a grace-filled preparation for what death may hold: a reunion with the source and summation of all that is! Something in us still clamors for personal survival in some recognizable form, but there is also in us what there was in Jung—a "still small voice" within that is willing to forego this last frenetic plea of the ego and to "let go" with confidence and trust into the "homecoming." This trust can be born of an experience such as the poet Kathleen Raine describes for us at an earlier period of life:

> There was also a hyacinth in an amethyst glass; I was sitting alone in an evening at my table, the Aladdin lamp lit, the fire of logs burning on the hearth. All was stilled. I was looking at the hyacinth, and as I gazed at the form of its petals and strength of their curve as they opened and curled back to reveal the mysterious flower-center with their anthers and eye-like hearts, abruptly I found I was no longer looking *at* it, but *was* it; a distinct, indescribable, but in no way vague, still less emotional, shift of consciousness into the plant itself . . . I dared scarcely to breathe, held in a kind of fine attention in which I could sense the very flow of life in the cells. I was not perceiving the flower but living it. I was aware of this life of the plant as a slow flow of circulation of a vital current of liquid light of the utmost purity . . . There was nothing emotional about this experience which was, on the contrary, an almost mathematical apprehension of a complex and organized whole, apprehended as a whole. This whole was living; and as such inspired a sense of immaculate holiness . . . The experience lasted for some time, I have no idea how

long, and I returned to dull commonplace consciousness with a sense of diminution. I had never before experienced the like, nor have I since in the same degree; yet it seemed at the time not strange but infinitely familiar, as if I were experiencing at last things as they are, was where I belonged, where in some sense, I had always been and would always be. That almost continuous sense of exile and incompleteness of experience which is, I suppose, the average human state, was gone like a film from sight. In these matters to know once is to know forever.

Something comparable to Kathleen Raine's experience probably most of us have had in one form or another. In the context in which we have been reflecting, such an experience would seem to be a kind of precognition of reabsorption into the all which may be our lot at death. It would not preserve and foster our ego-consciousness. Quite the contrary! But in the divine economy it may serve much more altruistic ends.

Dreams and Death

Marie-Louise von Franz, a student and colleague of C.G. Jung, has produced a very interesting study on dreams and death. In her research she discovered that flowers have often been an archetypal image of the "postmortal" existence of the soul, a symbol of life that survives death. She suggests that in the Jungian point of view, the flower points to the Self, the inner psychic totality.

In this sense the flower is a slowly maturing inner core, a totality into which the soul withdraws after death.

Other symbols that appear in dreams and represent post-mortal existence are the star and the bird. She notes that in German and Swiss mythologies the appearance in a dream of a black dog presages the death of someone. Jung records being visited by such a dream the night his mother died:

I was in a dense, gloomy forest . . . It was a heroic, primeval landscape. Suddenly I heard a piercing whistle. My knees shook. Then there were crashings in the underbush, and a gigantic wolfhound with a fearful, gaping maw burst forth. It tore past me, and I suddenly knew: the Wild Huntsman had commanded it to carry away a human soul. . . . The next morning I received the news of my mother's passing.

To Jung the dream clearly said that the soul of his mother

was taken into that greater territory of the Self . . . into that wholeness of nature and spirit in which conflicts and contradictions are resolved . . .

Von Franz calls attention to an important conviction of Jung's:

Jung suggests that in the deepest layers of the unconscious, which seem to be spaceless and timeless, there prevails a relative eternality, and a relative non-separation from other psyches, or a oneness with them.

From which von Franz concludes,

Death and Self—God's image, that is—are de facto indistinguishable.

This would support our earlier point that consciousness at death may be assimilated in a new mystical union with God. The unconscious milieu and the milieu into which consciousness is assimilated at death are one. This milieu can be imaged as infinity, and the more one remains sensitive to the infinitive, that is, the more one consciously lives one's life "under the aspect of the eternal," here and now, the more one is inwardly prepared to die.

Jung insisted that a certain part of the psyche is not confined to the space-time continuum. It is capable of telepathic and precognitive perceptions, as we have already noted. But we are incapable of knowing about existence outside of time. It may be, he suggests, that there is an existence outside of time that runs parallel with existence inside time. Perhaps we may exist simultaneously in both worlds. He observes that the unconscious strives to prepare consciousness for a continuation of the life process, but concedes that "this is unimaginable to everyday consciousness."

Dying Gracefully

Teilhard cherished the desire, as he put it, "to make a good end." To him this meant retaining consciousness to the last moment, being unafraid, and committing himself confidently into God's keeping, knowing that with God all things are well. There is a legend in the Catholic Church to the effect that if one should die while receiving communion the soul would go immediately to heaven. Familiar with this tradition, Teilhard turns it into a nobler aspiration. He writes in *The Divine Milieu*

It is not enough that I should die while communicating. Teach me to treat my death as an act of communion.

He had often said to his friends that he hoped he might die on Easter Day. He was granted this wish. On Easter Day in 1955, having gone to Mass in the morning at St. Patrick's Cathedral, he attended an informal string quartet concert with a few friends in the afternoon, and while at tea with them afterward, in the act of serving one of them, he fell forward and died. His last words were, "This time it's terrible," clearly distinguishing this experience from an earlier heart attack. He knew he was dying. His long inward preparation for death stood him in good stead. He made a very good end.

A book, *Living Your Dying*, suggests that it is possible to program one's own death, that at least now and again, with a well-individuated person, the psychosomatic unity is such that the body is responsive to the psyche in this desire. Certainly Teilhard's would seem to be a case in point. Death is a moment of supreme opportunity for raised consciousness, to return the gift of life to the Giver of life. It is also an opportunity to bestow on one's family and friends a final gift, making the manner of one's "going" a thing of beauty and grace.

What I have been trying to suggest is that we are in a period of transition when many of us have had to forego the comfort and reassurance of traditional myths of immortality, and there has not yet emerged from the unconscious a new and viable myth of the meaning of death. We are no longer able to accept the myth of the resurrection of the body, dependent for its validation on an empty tomb. We are entreated by friends to embrace with faith the testimony to personal survival by mediums, spiritualists, those who engage in channeling, those who have had vivid experiences in the interlude between being pronounced dead and returning to life, and those who are persuaded of the reality of reincarnation. While we are impressed and may sometimes be envious of their beliefs, integrity constrains us to confess that we are in fact unconvinced. In our attempt to assimilate into our personal myth of meaning fresh revelation emanating from the fact of evolution and the accumulating wisdom emerging from depth psychology, we have had to acknowledge doubts and to formulate questions to which we have no answers.

We are also impressed by the approach of Michael Marsh in his attempt to weigh naturalistic evidence arising from the study of the brain with surgical experimentation and research. He has proposed the interesting hypothesis that the mind is greater than the physical brain, transcends it, indeed, and that the "pure memories" and "inmost self" for which no specific locus can be found in the brain may somehow reside in the mind and constitute that element in consciousness which may survive death. He attributes plausibility to this theory but concedes there is no way of knowing.

We welcome Wordsworth's contribution in his beautiful poem that draws upon the intimations derived from recollections of early childhood and the continuing witness of the inner child that accompanies us right into old age. "A little child shall lead them." We are prepared to listen to our own inner child whom we dimly recognize comes "trailing clouds of glory, from God who is our home." We acknowledge that in addition to experiences of unity with nature there is the whole infinite array of mystical experiences which afford us a sense of transcending, for the duration of the experience, the dimensions of space and time. These are immediate, here and now, experiences of eternity which bring us a firsthand, if fleeting, awareness of a different kind of time, "kairos," as distinct from "chronos." We concur with Jung when he suggests that we may exist in two worlds simultaneously, the world of biological space-time or duration and a world that is spaceless and timeless. Finally we accept the insight of the author of the Fourth Gospel: "This is life eternal, to know thee, the only true God and Jesus Christ whom thou hast sent." Life eternal, it may be, is a state of raised consciousness in which one knows herself or himself beloved of God and through obedience to God is released to love.

The clearest clue that the unconscious may be trying to help us prepare for death, we have suggested, is the sense that we are already one with all persons and all things and the readiness, at the same time, to offer up the self's most prized possession: an attainment of a measure of individuation. As many of the mystics say of their incommunicable experience, "I never was so much myself. I never was so completely beyond myself." Perhaps this in some sense is a foretaste of death. Be we cannot know. We have somehow to be able to let go even of our longing for personal survival of death by our loved ones and ourselves. I believe we are asked in this now moment, between old myths and the new universal myth that has not yet been born, to make the supreme gesture of letting go of our need for personal survival. We are asked to accept in utter trust the possibility that death may mean the very oblivion we so much fear.

To return this gift of consciousness to the Giver of consciousness, trusting that whatever disposition God makes of it will be well, to return my very being to my Creator in return for possible nonbeing, even so much is required of me! Can I rise to this level of detachment? Can I achieve this degree of magnanimity? Yes, I like to think it is just barely possible. I believe there is a narrow way that leads to this attainment of raised consciousness in this life. It is the way of contemplative prayer.

The practice of contemplative prayer is an opportunity to be prepared to die gracefully when the time comes. Contemplative prayer is practice in "letting go." This letting go is a means of learning to hallow our diminishments in order that in the end we may have learned how to hallow the great diminishment, death.

What most distinguishes life from non-life at this moment of death is breathing. It is not surprising, then, that at the threshold of the altered state of consciousness we call contemplation, one needs to follow one's breathing. There are many "ways in," but this is the classic one in all traditions. Following one's breathing is the highest common denominator, the royal entrance way to the contemplative state. Though the Eastern religions refer to contemplation as meditation whereas in the West we have reserved the name of meditation for that state of consciousness in which the mind is still engaged in discursive reasoning, East and West are quite in agreement as to the nature of the experience itself, whether called meditation or contemplation. In exchanging and sharing what can be said of their ultimately ineffable experience, mystics in both East and West use the same words to describe it: nothingness, darkness, the void, emptiness. These are the same words one would choose to describe aspects of what we most fear may await us in death: nothingness, darkness, the void, emptiness. Shall we not then practice little deaths on a daily basis in order to prepare ourselves for the Great Death?

First, one quiets the body because death involves a taking leave of the body. This may be done in a great variety of ways, including different forms of yoga practice. This is the easier part of the discipline. Most of us, with a little perseverance, can learn how to do this, though we shall use different techniques. What is most difficult is stilling the mind, staying the stream of consciousness in order to arrive at that suspended animation of thought which is the raised consciousness of contemplation.

There are countless ways of moving from focused consciousness to the diffuse awareness which is contemplation. One must experiment, beginning with the universal practice of following one's breathing, until one finds one's own way in. This may involve many failures and only a rare success. But once will do! The memory will never leave one as long as one lives. Moreover this heaven cannot be taken by storm. It is always a gift of grace. But one must do what one can. One can tidy one's little craft and hoist a sail. But one cannot make the wind of the spirit blow. "It bloweth where it listeth." We come by even the acceptance of the phenomena with a certain inward reluctance and disbelief. Our culture has so conditioned us that we actually are afraid of this unknown spacelessness and timelessness. We are frenetic by force of habit. The great contemplative Fénelon put it this way: "To hear the voice of the voiceless, one must be silent before her."

In this nothingness, darkness, void, emptiness one learns finally to let go. One with patience and perseverance can in time be transformed through contemplative prayer into a contemplative. Then one can confidently entrust one's being to the Creator, whatever death may bring! Whittier pointed the way. One can indeed "let go in love."

> I know not where his islands lift
> Their fronded palms in air.
> I only know I cannot drift
> Beyond God's love and care.

CHAPTER SEVEN

The Task of Shaping One's Own Myth

In conclusion we must draw a few threads together. I have given this book the title, *Shaping a Personal Myth to Live By*. A spirituality can never be identified as a particular aspect of one's life. It is all or nothing. In this respect it is like the self which insists on remaining the center as well as the whole of one's life. Of course, one's spirituality includes associations with earlier denominational membership. But it is the religion of one's soul, and therefore transcends the denomination and even the whole body of the Church as one of the living religions. Spirituality refers to what is holy in one's life and everything is potentially holy. Teilhard says rightly speaking, nothing is profane.

Spirituality as Energy Springing from Myth

Spirituality rightly springs from one's myth; this is what shapes the quality of one's spirituality. Remember that a myth, in a theological context, is a fabulous narrative about the early period of a people from which one learns about one's self, one's God, and the rest of creation. There are certain elements that a myth cannot leave out, that cry out for inclusion. It seems to me that the elements I have chosen for my personal myth are indispensable. I have arranged these, I hope, in an acceptable order.

A viable myth to support a new integrated spirituality would naturally begin with a story about creation. It would have to be a *new* story. The old story is no longer viable. But coming from our Christian heritage, most of us must answer afresh Jesus' query, "Who do you say that I am?" The second element is the appraisal of the value of man and woman, a new response to the ancient query, "What is man and woman that thou are mindful of them?" The third element has to do with the cultivation of the mystical faculty. The new spirituality must be inclusive of the immanent God without abandoning the idea of the transcendant God. The feminist revolution demands that the feminine at long last be granted its proper place in the theology of any religion. I have called that chapter, "The Eternal Feminine." Because the moral and theological teaching is so important and because we have recognized the importance of forgiveness, I have given a place to living into the forgiven life in my own personal myth of meaning. Finally, I have contemplated intimations of immortality as part of the myth of meaning for each one of us.

My own personal myth to live by, prodigiously condensed in its present form, is the following fabulous narrative: God so loved the world that God implanted in matter itself the seed which would one day, through continuing creation by evolution, give birth to the Christ life in one Jesus of Nazareth, thereby quickening the Christ seed in other men and women to their soul's salvation and fulfillment. This remythologizing of the traditional Christ myth is compatible with Darwin's *Origin of Species* and Teilhard's myth of cosmogenesis on the one hand, and the depth psychology of Freud and Jung on the other. All that serves individuation, the process of growing in wholeness, can assist in building one's myth along the lines that "follow the curve" of evolution.

Evolution, a Curve Which All Lines Must Henceforth Follow

The incarnation myth can be far more wonderful and comprehensive than was ever dreamed until now. The fresh revelation of the fact of evolution has infinitely expanded the meaning of the term "incarnation." The incarnation now must be understood not only as the presence of that of God in Jesus of Nazareth, but the Christ seed in every man and woman. The Christ seed was that of God at the heart of matter since the beginning of time, if one can speak of any ultimate beginning at all. The Christ potential is the most impressive diaphany of the divine at the heart of matter from the beginning, however it is to be conceived. In evolutionary perspective, the Christ life formed its finest expression to date in one Jesus of Nazareth, but is present in all men and women as a token of the "within" that

Teilhard envisioned. The Christ archetype of perfect manhood and womanhood dwells within everyone, containing the promise of the next step of human evolution. It is part of the process of human evolution, which will allow the movement toward Homo sapiens to become "Homo spiritus" in the course of continuing evolution.

The continuing movement toward higher consciousness is the forecast of Jesus ("Greater works than this shall ye do." John 14:12) Continuing creation must now replace the old myth of a completed creation in six days. We must reflect on what the pioneer scientists of our time are exploring in their research. Everything that is being created in the continuing process must "follow that curve" which constitutes the unfolding and ascending consciousness of the human being. Any growth of consciousness begins and moves forward with pain. They are almost identical—the more advanced the consciousness (awareness), the more intense the pain that must be endured. Indeed the cross that must be borne by the individual is his or her growing edge in consciousness. Another way of saying this is to point out that the inward journey to the self, which Jung called individuation, reveals itself as one and the same journey to the Self, God within.

Each one of us will experience his or her vision of continuing creation in a different way. So far Teilhard's vision, more than that of any other of our contemporary scientists, seems the most plausible to me. I embrace it and experiment with it in my continuing quest for a myth that is compatible with the best and most persuasive of contemporary research by those in the forefront in paleontology, astrophysics, quantum mechanics, and other scientific fields. It has been my good fortune to have known Leo Goldberg, astrophysicist at Harvard, until his untimely death. It must be clear, however, that as one goes back in time the ultimate source or beginning of creation recedes more and more, and there is a point at which our partial vision is blocked by a shroud of ultimate mystery. Even active imagination fails to reveal more at this time. I have the feeling that the next great revelation on this point of scientific exploration may be some new perception, perhaps arising from the unconscious of an astrophysicist. I am convinced that Teilhard, were he still living, would have rejoiced at the findings of those on the frontiers of science. Those studying subatomic particles find that a certain spontaneity, resembling a kind of primitive consciousness, exists at the heart of these particles. The embryo for spirit and consciousness lies in the heart of matter itself.

The Unconscious: The Only Accessible Source of Religious Experience

In his profound little book, *The Undiscovered Self*, written five years before his death, Jung gives expression to his deepest concern.

> The believer is no longer sustained by the tremendous suggestive power of the "consensus omnium," and is keenly aware of the weakening of the Church and the precariousness of its dogmatic assumptions. To counter this, the Church recommends more faith, as if this gift of grace depended upon man's good will and pleasure. The seat of faith, however, is not consciousness but spontaneous religious experience, which brings the individual's faith into immediate relation with God.
>
> Here we must ask: Have I any religious experience and immediate relation to God, and hence that certainty which will keep me, as an individual, from dissolving in the crowd?

Jung responds to his own query in this dramatic way:

> To this question there is a positive answer only when the individual is willing to fulfill the demands of rigorous self-examination and self-knowledge. If he follows through this intention he will not only discover some important truths about himself, but will also have gained a psychological advantage: he will have succeeded in deeming himself worthy of serious attention and sympathetic interest. He will have set his hand, as it were, to a declaration of his own human dignity and taken the first step towards the foundation of his consciousness—that is, towards the unconscious, the only accessible source of religious experience.

This suggests that images and symbols of one's myth of meaning emerge in dreams and mystical experiences from the unconscious. That is why it is so important to pursue the quest of a viable myth of meaning in cooperation with the unconscious. We need to learn to listen to and be respectful of its contents, especially in our dreams. To be attentive to our dreams and inner experiences, to work with them and labor to integrate their contents with consciousness, is one of our tasks. It is important as well to observe our spontaneous response in dialogue with others, perceiving what arouses our emotions. Jung explains the predicament of many modern men and women:

> So long as the individual can hold fast to his traditional beliefs, and the circumstances of his time do not demand strong emphasis on individual autonomy, he can rest content with the situation. But the situation is radically altered when the worldly-minded man who is oriented to external factors and has lost his religious beliefs appears en masse, as is

the case today. The believer is then forced onto the defensive and must catechise himself on the foundation of his beliefs.

In our time much is being written by scientists on creation as well as on the Anthropos. Anyone who is genuinely drawn "to a declaration of one's own human dignity" has a wealth of resources confirming his or her resolution to shape one's own myth of meaning, drawn by the aspiration to attain such measure of individuation as one is capable of, as distinct from pursuing the easier collective path. We have rich material at our disposal for study and for assisting us in questioning our own powers of reasoning. We have also a powerful tool in active imagination to access the unconscious and to assimilate its contents in response to dreams and fantasy. To shape one's own myth of meaning takes courage and perseverance. It is important not to assume that one can compartmentalize the psyche. Religion is the instinct to bind into one sheaf many strands, to "get it all together." We have commended Teilhard as mentor in the framework of cosmogenesis, the myth of ongoing creation, and C. G. Jung as mentor with regard to growing in wholeness, the process of integrating unconscious contents with consciousness, which he called individuation.

Cultivating the Mystical Faculty

Since the contemplative or mystical consciousness is universal and is the very growing edge of continuing creation, it helps to ask ourselves, "What kind of mystic am I?" and "What am I doing to cultivate this form of consciousness in my life?" No doubt Teilhard asked the same questions in his own effort to shape his personal myth of meaning. He must have steeped himself in the mystics. What has brought renewed significance to his work in our contemporary world is that he developed his mystical faculty with reference to identification with matter, and specifically with reference to the earth itself.

Two contemporary writers have served me well in this regard: Thomas Berry and Loren Eiseley. Thomas Berry, the author of *The Dream of the Earth*, published by the Sierra Club as the first of a series of a Nature Library, is a "Renaissance Man" with training in the sciences, including ecology, theology, cultural history, and philosophy. Loren Eiseley held the Benjamin Franklin chair at the University of Pennsylvania with its diversified portfolio in the sciences, including zoology, geology, paleontology, and botany. He also served as Provost for a time. Despite his vast learning in these fields, he aspired to be a literary naturalist in the succession of Thoreau, Muir, and others, and succeeded in winning that place for himself. In his books he describes instance after instance of communion with nature in a deep sharing with his readers. They amount to an earth mysticism. Eiseley died some years ago, and there has been no replacement for one as gifted in revealing how to go about cultivating the mystical faculty in relation to nature. Eiseley all his life worked on shaping his own myth of meaning. He has much reticence in articulating it, preferring to yield to the ultimate mysteries of life without pressing them into a mould that would serve any collective. That is why we owe him so much. He has shown us the path of an earth mysticism, while respecting the demand that the process of individuation imposes on each of us for our own originality based on experience. Nevertheless, Thomas Berry and Loren Eiseley remain great mentors in leading the way.

One must find his or her own way into building a personal myth of meaning, but a study of the works of these nature mystics can get us started and point us in the right direction. Both are indebted to Teilhard for their initial instruction and resolve. I am deliberately limiting myself to a few suggestions. The important thing is to choose the way of mysticism and to get started on this royal road, and to join the apostolic succession of the mystics which has included from the beginning women as well as men. Those who would become mystics or contemplatives will commit themselves to the discipline of contemplation by letting go into the darkness, the void, the emptiness, the nothingness. There they may confirm in part, through the Holy Spirit, their personal myth of meaning as they touch the source.

The Eternal Feminine

No myth can be viable, I believe, without consciously having an adequate place for the eternal feminine. In the last decade there has sprung up vast literature on this theme with demands for inclusive language and inclusive theological statements in the Church. In another vein, books written by Irene Claremont de Castillejo and Helen Luke contain the deepest kind of philosophical insights. Men constantly reveal their need for growth in sensitivity on this issue. In response to the Feminist Movement, fine books are now written on the masculine psyche, such as *Iron John* by Robert Bly. There is a need for men's groups as well as women's groups.

On Living Into the Forgiven Life

I would encourage the reader to go back to the gospels with Blake's query in mind and see if the originality in Jesus' teaching lies in the emphasis he placed on forgiveness, as Blake claimed. Does it coincide with your ideas concerning forgiveness, and have you tested its authenticity? The Twelve Step program confirms the pathway of forgiveness to release love. Recall the statement in the New Testament, often repeated, "If you forgive one another, your heavenly Father will also forgive you." (Matthew 6:14) Is God inhibited from forgiving us until we forgive one another? This is what a number of passages clearly say. And perhaps we find it hardest of all to forgive ourselves or to accept forgiveness from another. Once more the Twelve Step programs offer us insight. We can forgive ourselves for twenty-four hours. Then we can forgive ourselves for another twenty-four hours. I feel it necessary to include in my personal myth of meaning the importance of living in twenty-four-hour encapsulated days.

Intimations of Immortality

Earlier in this book I dealt with the problem of death and preparing to die. I confess that I am not persuaded of personal survival after death by those who reported their experience of being pronounced dead and of then returning to the land of the living. There is always the possibility that such an experience emanates from the personal or the collective unconscious. This same uncertainty applies to spiritualism and channeling. For me the most persuasive intimations of immortality derive from mystical experience in which we feel a certain timelessness, as if we had transcended this plane. At such moments we seem to experience life eternal. This, taken with the experience (at the heart of all mystical religion) that we are loved unconditionally, without reservations or restrictions, by the great Presence, gives me the confidence to place myself in the hands of the Source that gave me birth, in perfect trust that the love that brought me into being can be trusted to dispose of me in whatever way God chooses. Yea, though God assign me to oblivion, yet will I love God. "All shall be well, and all shall be well, and all shall be very well."

Select Bibliography

Episcopal Church. *The Book of Common Prayer, Nicene Creed.* New York: J. Pott & Co., 1929.

Aurobindo, Sri. *The Life Divine: A Commentary on Isha Upanished.* India: Sri Aurobindo Ashram Trust, 1981.

Berry, Thomas. *The Dream of the Earth.* San Francisco: Sierra Club Books, 1988.

Blake, William. "The Everlasting Gospel." In *William Blake: A Selection of Poems and Letters.* Baltimore, MD: Penguin Books, 1958.

Blakney, Raymond Bernard. *Meister Eckhart: A Modern Translation.* New York: Harper & Brothers, 1941.

Bly, Robert. *Iron John.* Reading, MA: Addison-Wesley, 1990.

Burney, Pierre. "Sketch for a Morality of Love: A Tentative Application of Teilhardian Methods" *Perspective II.*

Campbell, Joseph. *The Power of Myth.* New York: Doubleday, 1988.

Capra, Fritjof. *The Tao of Physics.* Boulder, CO: Shambala Publications, 1975.

Darwin, Charles. *Origin of Species.* New York: Collier, 1937.

De Castillejo, Irene Claremont. *Knowing Woman.* New York: Harper and Row, 1973.

DeCaussade, Jean-Pierre. *Abandonment to Divine Providence.* New York: Doubleday, 1975.

De Gourmont, Remy. *Physique de l'Amour.* Paris: AMS Press, 1940.

De Lubac, Henri. *Teilhard de Chardin, A Man and His Meaning.* New York: Mentor-Omega Books, 1967.

Eiseley, Loren. *The Immense Journey.* New York: Random House, 1957.

Fox, Matthew. *Original Blessing.* Santa Fe, NM: Bear & Co., 1983.

Frost, Robert. "Birches." In *Selected Poems.* Great Britain: Penguin Books, 1955.

Frost, Robert. "Education by Poetry." In *Teaching and Learning*. New York: Ethical Culture School, 1960.

Hanh, Thich Nhat. *The Miracle of Mindfulness*. Boston: Beacon Press, 1987.

Inge, William Ralph. *Christian Mysticism*. London: Methven & Co., 1989.

Jacobi, Jolande. *Masks of the Soul*. Grand Rapids, MI: William B. Eerdmans Publishing Company, 1976.

John, M.P. *In Defense of Death*. Pondicherry, India: Jyotishikha Press, 1989.

Johnston, William. *The Inner Eye of Love: Mysticism and Religion*. San Francisco: Harper & Row, 1978.

Jung, C.G. *Answer to Job*. Princeton, NJ: Princeton University Press, 1973.

Jung, C.G. *Memories, Dreams, Reflections*. New York: Pantheon Books, 1963.

Jung, C.G. *The Undiscovered Self*. Boston: Little, Brown & Co., Inc., 1957.

Keleman, Stanley. *Living Your Dying*. Berkeley, CA: Center Press, 1985.

Marsh, Michael. *A Matter of Personal Survival: Life After Death*. Wheaton, IL: The Theosophical Publishing House, 1985.

Neumann, Erich. *Amor and Psyche: The Psychic Development of the Feminine*. Princeton, NJ: Princeton University Press, 1956.

Raine, Kathleen. *The Presence: Poems Nineteen Eighty-Four to Nineteen Eighty-Nine*. Hudson, NY: Lindisfarne Press, 1987.

Steere, Douglas. *Mutual Irradiation: A Quaker View of Ecumenism*. Wallingford, PA: Pendle Hill Publications, 1971.

Swimme, Brian. *The Universe is A Green Dragon: A Cosmic Creation Story*. Santa Fe, NM: Bear & Co., 1984.

Teilhard de Chardin, Pierre. *The Divine Milieu*. New York: Harper and Row, 1960.

Teilhard de Chardin, Pierre. *The Heart of Matter*. New York: Harcourt Brace Jovanovich, 1978.

Teilhard de Chardin, Pierre. *The Phenomenon of Man*. New York: Harper & Row, 1959.

Teilhard de Chardin, Pierre. *Toward the Future*. New York: Harcourt Brace Jovanovich, 1975.

Tennyson, Alfred Lord. "Flower in the Crannied Wall." In *Immortal Poems*. New York: Pocket Books, Inc., 1957.

von Franz, Marie-Louise. *On Dreams and Death*. Boston: Shambhala Publications, Inc., 1986.

Walker, Susan, ed. *Speaking of Silence: Christians and Buddhists on the Contemplative Way*. New York: Paulist Press, 1987.

Wheelwright, Jane Hollister. "Old Age and Death." In *Betwixt and Between*. La Salle, IL: Open Court, 1987.'

Whittier, John Greenleaf. "The Eternal Goodness." In *The Complete Poetical Works of John Greenleaf Whittier*. Boston: Houghton Mifflin and Co., 1985.

Wordsworth, William. "Lines Composed a Few Miles Above Tintern Abbey." In *Complete Poetical Works*. Boston: Houghton Mifflin Co., 1932.

Wordsworth, William. "Lines Composed a Few Miles Above Tintern Abbey." In *Complete Poetical Works*. Boston: Houghton Mifflin Co., 1932.

Yungblut, John. *The Gentle Art of Spiritual Guidance*. Amity, NY: Amity House, Inc., 1988.

Zukav, Gary. *The Dancing Wu Li Masters: An Overview of the New Physics*. New York: William Morrow & Co., Inc. 1979.